LEADING FROM THE HEART

LEADING FROM THE HEART

Sufi Principles at Work

Moid Siddiqui

SAGE | Response Business Books

www.sagepublications.com

Los Angeles • London • New Delhi • Singapore • Washington DC

First published in 2014 by

SAGE Response
B1/I-1 Mohan Cooperative Industrial Area
Mathura Road, New Delhi 110 044, India

SAGE Publications Inc
2455 Teller Road
Thousand Oaks, California 91320, USA

SAGE Publications Ltd
1 Oliver's Yard, 55 City Road
London EC1Y 1SP, United Kingdom

SAGE Publications Asia-Pacific Pte Ltd
3 Church Street
#10-04 Samsung Hub
Singapore 049483

Published by Vivek Mehra for SAGE Publications India Pvt Ltd, typeset in 11/14 Baskerville by Diligent Typesetter, Delhi and printed at **Sai Print O Pack.** Pvt Ltd, New Delhi.

Library of Congress Cataloging-in-Publication Data Available

ISBN: 978-81-321-1370-6 (PB)

The SAGE Team: Sachin Sharma, Prasenjit Paul, Nand Kumar Jha and Rajinder Kaur

I dedicate this book to a person dear to my heart—my uncle Janab Syed Masood Hasan. His character soaked in simplicity and his identity cloaked in humility makes him the only person I would revere, to be gifted with *Sufi sagacity*.

He is an upright *tabligi* (Islamic Missionary), whom I have never seen preach—his own way of life is an eloquent sermon. He wears simple attire yet holds the jewel in his heart.

To Masood Mamu, who has been an enigma during my youth, and an inspiration in gaining spiritual maturity!

Thank you for choosing a SAGE product! If you have any comment, observation or feedback, I would like to personally hear from you. Please write to me at contactceo@sagepub.in

—Vivek Mehra, Managing Director and CEO,
SAGE Publications India Pvt Ltd, New Delhi

Bulk Sales

SAGE India offers special discounts for purchase of books in bulk. We also make available special imprints and excerpts from our books on demand.

For orders and enquiries, write to us at

Marketing Department
SAGE Publications India Pvt Ltd
B1/I-1, Mohan Cooperative Industrial Area
Mathura Road, Post Bag 7
New Delhi 110044, India
E-mail us at marketing@sagepub.in

Get to know more about SAGE, be invited to SAGE events, get on our mailing list. Write today to marketing@sagepub.in

This book is also available as an e-book.

CONTENTS

Foreword by R.H. Khwaja *ix*
Preface *xi*

1. Sufi Sagacity in Leadership 3
2. Leadership with Secular Approach 15
3. Leadership Consciousness: Know Thyself 27
4. Journey from 'Head' to 'Heart' 37
5. Leading 'Inside-out' 49
6. Reach the Heart with 'High-Touch' 61
7. Stop Chasing the Mirage 73
8. Generosity in Leadership 91
9. Managing 'Conflicting Perspectives' 103
10. Develop a Heart That Can Trust 117
11. Marinate Leadership in Humility 129
12. Law of Energy Response 137
13. Build the Ark First 147
14. Leader and the Led 153
15. Be a Melody Maker 159
16. The Art of 'Wu Wei' 165
17. 'Main Hoon Na...' Is Empowerment 173
18. Lead with a Sufi Heart: 'Dil Se' 179

About the Author *191*

FOREWORD

I have once again submitted to the direction of Management Monk Moid Siddiqui in penning this foreword for his latest masterpiece *Leading from the Heart—Sufi Principles at Work*. As Moid's co-author of *The Acrobatics of Change* (2008), I was launched as an author entirely due to his motivation, guidance and inspiration. For unfathomable reasons, Moid sahib continues to embarrass me by heaping praises on me which I do not deserve. However, for me his wish is always a command and I consider it a great privilege and honour to write the foreword of this book.

I have gone through the draft of *Leading from the Heart*. I find my heart and soul in supreme harmony with the central theme of this book, which can be encapsulated in the following extract:

> *Fill your heart with so much love and passion that there remains no place for hatred. For this you are required to undertake a great journey—a journey from your head to heart. The common DNA of all great leaders is they travelled from head to heart, they lead from within.*

I strongly recommend the approach of this book, which focuses on learning from Sufism. The emphasis on secularism, journey from head to heart, marinating leadership in humility and leading from inside out are compelling, lyrical and over-powering. Moid sahib has consistently focused on the human aspects of management in today's crassly materialistic environment where the predominant value is to be 'value-less'. The relevance of Moid will grow exponentially as we witness further degradation of human actions. Like a true pioneer, Moid continues to relentlessly walk a narrow, dark and treacherous path, constantly singing hymns till his tongue bleeds for upholding the values of humanism, secularism, spiritualism and Sufism.

We all grapple with contradictions and paradoxes in our daily existence on planet earth. Sadly, we are witnessing constant deterioration in the moral fibre of human society. The true Sufi is one who never gives up, no matter what the odds. Moid is a genuine Sufi who has written books with titles like *Corporate Soul, Soul Inc.* and *50 Soul Stories*. His writings relentlessly reinforce moral values and these are powerfully brought out in *Leading from the Heart*.

It is my fond hope that this book will reach the widest possible range of readers. This is '*A Must Read Book*' for all persons who are engaged in genuine efforts of self-improvement and in battling nearly insurmountable challenges in day-to-day life. Books continue to be one of the most powerful tools for gaining knowledge and wisdom. It is my sincere hope that *Leading from the Heart* will inspire all those who read it and contribute to their inner awakening. The awakened readers will then make consistent and serious efforts to change their value systems. The changed value systems will be reflected in their changed actions. Only then the cycle will be complete.

I conclude this foreword with the fervent appeal to readers of this book to always spot the glow worms in the pitch darkness of hopelessness. We should lead 'from the Heart'. We should be part of the solution and not the problem. We should attempt to see the divine light in this enveloping darkness. If this happens, Moid would have succeeded in his noble mission of imparting Sufi values in today's *kalyug*.

May all readers take their first tentative and unsure steps as they embark on the journey of *Leading from the Heart* based on the values on Sufism. I strongly recommend this book to all readers who are prepared to accept and unleash their inherent nobility. We should all regenerate our innate sense of goodness and justice and crush negative and materialistic values. Let us all attempt to lead *from the Heart*.

R.H. Khwaja
Secretary, Ministry of Mines, Government of India

PREFACE

The ancient Indian sages called the era in which we live today as *Kali Yuga* (age of the demon or the age of vices). As per Indian scriptures, this is the last of four stages the world goes through as part of the cycle of *yuga*s. The other ages are *Satya Yuga, Treta Yuga* and *Dvapara Yuga*. What the ancient sages could see, our eyes cannot see. But nothing prevents us pondering upon: *Are we not living in the era where something strange is happening—profane is taken as pure and sacred is mistaken as sordid?*

There are two ways to think and shape our approach—*Surrender* or *Strive!* I have opted for the latter. Our job is to build the Ark before the Deluge strikes. God helps those who help themselves. God bends the heavens and paves the path with success for those who demonstrate courage. Who built the Ark? Noah—the leader of the community. A single leader could save the entire community. Leaders are important. The corrupted leaders can corrupt the world and corporate world; the honest leaders can protect the world and corporate world with their sagacity. Sufi Sagacity is the need of the day.

Our sages, saints and Sufis never defy. What they said hundreds of years back, today we are witnessing the degeneration in societies. The pace of value-corruption is fast, which is accelerating with every cockcrow. What didn't happen in eons has happened in the recent past few decades! I wonder if this is happening by chance! Well, to me, just like a crazy monkey by mindlessly pressing the keys of the keyboard cannot create a poem of Shakespeare, the events shaping our worlds are but a well-articulated master plan.

Since the degeneration is taking place at the level of leadership, the corrective measures should also be taken at the same level. Hence this attempt to rekindle the soul of leadership, through this book *Leading from the Heart: Sufi Principles at Work*.

I recognise it is not easy to sell the truth with sweet words. Lao Tzu—the Old Master—said over 2,500 years back: 'Truthful words are not beautiful and beautiful words are not truthful.' The readers will sometime find some of the text punctuated with harsh words and loud viewpoints, which, in fact, contains medicinal value.

The architect of the problems cannot become the Messiah. Nevertheless, today it is happening. Sitting on the riches of the ill-gotten coffers, many corrupt leaders sermonise their people to leave corruption. Those who are unchaste preach people to be chaste. Further, some political leaders try to seek solution through legislation. They understand not that the problems of such high magnitude cannot be solved through legislative resolutions. This will not grind until we go to the root of the problem. For this reason we need Sufi Sagacity in leadership. Going to the roots is an art that we can learn from Kung Fu Tzu (Confucius). If the leaders want to understand their people, there is no other root to reach them except through the heart. If the leaders want their people to be virtuous, first they have to fill their hearts with love and wisdom.

Wishing to illustrate 'illustrious virtue' through out the kingdom,
They first ordered well their own states.
Wishing to order well their own states,
They first regulated their families.
Wishing to regulate their families,
They first cultivated their persons.
Wishing to cultivate their persons,
They first rectified their hearts.
Wishing to rectify their hearts,
They first sought to be sincere in their thoughts.
Wishing to be sincere in their thoughts,
They first extended to the utmost their knowledge.
Such extension of knowledge lays investigation of things.
Things being investigated, knowledge became complete.

—*Confucius*

Hence, if the world has to change, we need to redevelop leadership with Sufi Sagacity. Today we do not need management gurus, we need management monks. It is time we realise that we need more than intellects or knowledge in the corporate world; we need wisdom and virtue in its leadership. Yes! It takes time to grow in wisdom, yet sometimes wisdom comes in unexpected flashes. 'Everyday, God gives us the sun—and also one moment in which we have ability to change everything,' believes Paulo Coelho, the author of *The Alchemist*. Those who capture this moment of truth become monks.

Not *logic* but the *intuitive wisdom* will get readers its real flavour. Neither *transactional leadership*, nor *transformational leadership*, but *leadership with Sufi's Sagacity* is the model of tomorrow. Before imparting sagacity unto others, leaders must first kindle their hearts with Sufi Sagacity. It is a long journey, beyond the stock price or quarterly profits. This toil is but a one small step towards that direction the social and corporate worlds need to travel.

This earnest work is worthy of your concentration—my words are simple to understand but not those that come from Sufis quoted herein. It is not quite easy to understand the Sufi wisdom: 'A child has no real knowledge of the attainments of an adult. An ordinary adult cannot understand the attainments of a learned man. In the same way, an educated man cannot yet understand the experience of enlightened saints and Sufis,' cautions the great Sufi Al-Ghazali. Sufism is an interesting subject—Sufi thoughts are bottomless deep.

The purpose of this book is to sensitise the hearts and fill the souls of managers and leaders with Sufi Sagacity. This book stands to rebuild confidence in the ancient values, virtues and wisdom, which are distancing from us with the passage of time. This book will (God willing) help you in taking a sharp U-turn from *what we think is good* to *what is really good*. 'If all they say of good and evil were true, then my life is but one long crime,' says Kahlil Gibran, a great Sufi of Lebanon. Whatever is happening today in the name of modernisation is not good. The purpose of this book is to re-mind and revive the forgotten ancient values. Readers will gain enormous benefit from the age-old values, which, in turn, will help them in rekindling their hearts, and soul of their organisations.

'When the country is confused and in darkness, loyal minsters appear,' believes the Old Master—Lao Tzu. The glow worms appear only in thick dark nights.

Let us not look at the darkness; let us look at the glow-worms—the *loyal ministers*. There is no cause of despair—in the heart of *dusk* lives *dawn*. *Leading Dil Se* is the glow worm, which will kindle the heart of leadership.

Leading Dil Se is the call of time—we can thrive only when virtuous leaders take charge.

Moid Siddiqui

Go beyond language; go beyond thought.

—*Buddha*

1

SUFI SAGACITY IN LEADERSHIP

To come empty-handed to the door of friends is like going to the mill without wheat.
—JELALUDDIN RUMI, *RUMI DAYLIGHT—A DAYBOOK OF SPIRITUAL GUIDANCE*

Gone are the days when *Sufi Sagacity* and *Leadership* lived like twin sisters. They were like two loving hearts, made for each other. But today, one may wonder, how can they coexist? They have separated and drifted away with the flow of time. Like step sisters, they cannot dwell together in the same heart. It seems there is no matching point between them. But bringing them together is necessary. Their coexistence is the need of time.

Where have we gone wrong? Changing the focus from *spirituality* to *materialism* was the drifting point. In anxiety to keep the entire focus on *excellence*, in terms of material gains, we have killed the spirit of leadership by gradually discarding its softer aspects relating to values, virtue and sagacity. Earlier the pace of deterioration was slow, but of late it has picked up the speed. I can notice the difference during my lifetime itself. During my corporate life of four decades, I find a sea of change—people talk about values and virtues shallowly, without demonstrating them in leadership practices. Coming to political leadership, I find a vast difference between the leadership of the times of Indian independence and today. Both political and corporate leadership quality is regressing in terms of values on fast pace. Exceptions are always there but exceptions cannot be taken as totality. I can quote many incidents.

I recollect an anecdote that was shared with me by the former President of India, Dr Shanakardayal Sharma, about the clean government of Pandit Jawaharlal Nehru. I knew Dr Shankardayal Sharma from the times he was a professor at Hamidia College, Bhopal, from where I have graduated. It was amazing to hear from him that once Pandit Nehru noticed one of his cabinet ministers wearing an *imported watch*. During those days, as per the policy of the government, *import* of watches was not permissible. Obviously, the minister was wearing a watch that was smuggled to India. Next day, the minister tendered his resignation on the advice of Pandit Nehru. Those were the days of good governance, though this phraseology was non-existent as a buzzword. Later, Lal Bahadur Shastri led the country holding ancient Indian values and sagacity. As days passed by, the political values started decaying. When termites eat up a major portion, what remains is the decomposed structure, which can collapse anytime. I am talking about the entire political system of the country, not mere the leadership in power. When the entire political system gets corrupted, what choice is left with the voters?

Those were the golden days of my country, India! Had the later politicians followed the earlier governance, India would not have taken the path of corruption. Today, the scams and corrupt practices have replaced the governance values. Most astonishingly, the gross domestic product (GDP) is increasing and people are becoming poorer! Reason: Earlier the size of scams was smaller, today it is huge. Time has changed, and so changed the values! The scene of corporate India is no different.

Today, *leadership* has lost its soul—Sufi Sagacity is missing in leadership. To understand *Sufi Sagacity*, one needs to understand first *Who is Sufi?* To understand Sufi, one must understand the meaning of Sufism. So, let me begin with Sufism, not elaborately but briefly.

Sufism is also known as mysticism or *bhakti* (soul power or spirituality). In Arabic and Persian, there are many words for Sufi—*fakir* (who renunciates worldly pleasures), *dervish* (spiritual person), *majzub* (lover of God). The sign of a true Sufi is that he feels poor when he has wealth, is humble when he has power and is hidden when he has fame. The sign of the false Sufi is that he acts rich towards the world when he is poor, acts powerful when he is powerless and tries to attain fame to triumph over his anonymity. Are the signs of a true leader and misleader anyway different?

A true Sufi is one who hides and prefers anonymity to popularity. Worldly riches, power and position are worthless. He understands that *greatness is not in exalted positions; greatness is for he who refuses position*. For Sufis, wealth and gold are worthless. They know, 'Gold leads into gold, then into restlessness and finally into crushing misery. The life that the rich man spends in heaping gold is in truth like the life of the worms in the grave.' Worldly riches create perturbation in life. Richness is a disease, which leads to many diseases in morality. Sufi's richness lies in their hearts. Their body is poor but soul is rich.

> **Divine Trust**
>
> Knock, and He will open the door;
>
> Vanish, and He will make you shine like the sun;
>
> Fall, and He will raise you to the glorious height;
>
> Become nothing, and He will turn you into everything.
> —Jelaluddin Rumi, *RUMI Daylight—A Daybook of Spiritual Guidance*

As mentioned, Sufism, *bhakti* and mysticism are three names of the same spiritual transcendence—get linked with God directly without any intervention or specific way of meditation. All these three roads lead to the same destination. Sufis, mystics or sages are the enlightened beings who are capable of establishing bonds with the Superior Being directly.

Al-Ghazali was a great Sufi and philosopher of 12th century. He authored many books and many of his saying caught currency.

The Westerners were very much influence by his thoughts and philosophy. His contribution to human thought and the relevance of his ideas even after hundreds of years remained unquestioned.

The 13th century witnessed another great Sufi who was known for his uniqueness of teachings. He used to draw wisdom upon people through his *foolhardiness*. Yes, it was Mulla Nasrudin, the starring character in a vast number of amusing tales told in regions all over the world, particularly in counties in or near the Middle East. Each tale depicts Nasrudin in a different situation, and through his viewpoint they humorously reveal commentary and lessons on various life-themes. The great allure of the Mulla Nasrudin tales is that they are funny as well as lesson filled, philosophical and thought-provoking. In uniqueness, Mulla Nasrudin stands out—there is no comparable Sufi who can match his *naughty* retorts filled with sagacity.

Speaking truth and accepting truth is not all that easy. Mulla Nasrudin was known for his wits and sharpness. He was a great Sufi whose thoughts and acts many could not comprehend. He was witty yet a man of great wisdom. Let me quote one of anecdotes, which depicts his simplicity and sagacity:

> *The village mayor wrote a poem and read it to Nasrudin.*
> *'Did you like the poem?' he asked.*
> *'No, not really,' Nasrudin replied, 'it wasn't very good.'*
> *The mayor was enraged, and he sentenced Nasrudin to three days in jail. The next week, the mayor called Nasrudin in his office to read him another poem he had written. When the mayor finished reading, he turned to Nasrudin and asked, 'Well, what do you think of this one?'*
> *Nasrudin did not say anything, and immediately began walking away. The mayor inquired, 'Just where do you think you're going?'*
> *'To jail!' Nasrudin replied.*[1]

Truthfulness is an essentiality in leadership. It needs both, courage and guts. 'Buttering the royal toast' and 'speaking what creates music to the royal ears' is anything but leadership.

[1] Mullah Nasrudin, *The Outrageous Wisdom of Nasrudin.*

Sufis speak the truth in plain words, yet people do not understand the truth, because they do not take Sufis seriously due to their deceptive appearance. Showmanship is not leadership. Public Relations (PR) agency cannot create leaders. Overprojection rather distorts the image. A real leader never claims him as a great leader. True leadership lies in one's sagacity, simplicity and humility. Arrogance and egotism have no place in leadership.

Perhaps the most common epithets for the Sufis were drawn from the vocabulary of love and

Wilful Denunciation

My words are easy to understand and easy to perform; Yet no man under the heaven knows them or practice them. My words have ancient beginnings; My actions are disciplined. Because men do not understand, they have no knowledge of me. Those that know me are few; Those that abuse me are honoured. Therefore the sage wears rough clothing and holds the jewel in his heart.

—Lao Tzu, *Tao Te Ching*

infinite affection. Sufis are known as the true lovers of God. Intoxicated with divine love, they grow in divine madness. They know the inner truth. They discover universe within. They are humble to their knowledge. They understand their limitations. They strongly believe that they know not the entire truth. They know to the extent God has desired to reveal to them. They know they do not know many things in this universe: 'Some things are not favoured by Heaven; Who knows why? Even the Sage is unsure of this!'.[2] Are these qualities of Sufis not meaningful and desirable for true leadership, where love and service to people should be the driving force, not the power and material gains?

Leaders can learn a lot from the sagacity of the sages and the Sufis and grow as a true leader. Who is the true leader? 'He who takes upon himself the humiliation of the people is fit to rule them,' says Lao Tzu. He adds, 'He who takes upon the country's disasters deserves to be the king of the universe. The truth often

[2] Lao Tzu, *Tao Te Ching*.

sounds paradoxical.' There are many musclemen who are in race to emerge as the global leaders. How many of them stand near to Lao Tzu's defined leadership standards?

Taking blames and giving credit are the art of leadership that one must learn from the sagacity of sages and Sufis. When you get success, open the window and look for someone to give the credit. When you meet the failure, look into the mirror to own the responsibility.

Today all this seems to be some sort of fairytales. This is because we dwell in the world and corporate world, which have gone corrupt and their souls are sold out for material gains. But, believe me, leading with a Sufi Heart was in practice in various parts of the world. In ancient days in many countries the sages were the kings. I can quote the examples of these sages from different parts of the world at different cuts of time.

In 13th century BC, after Exodus from Egypt, and wandering 40 years in wilderness, when Jews recaptured Canaan under the leadership of Joshua, initially there was neither a king nor any kingdom. They lived independently as 12 separate tribes. Then began the period known in Israeli history as 'The Days when Judges Ruled'. 'Judges'—Jewish Saints and Sufis—were considered as the representatives of God. The saintly headers used to guide people through their pious hearts filled with love for people. The last sage, who ruled Jerusalem, was Samuel, a Jewish sage. During his time, all the 12 Jewish tribes were together—this period, which lasted until King Saul was installed in the year 1025 BC, was considered the Golden Period in the history of Israel. Even after King Saul, King David and King Solomon ruled the country with utmost care of people. The downfall of Jewish history begins with the end of Solomon Kingdom.

Likewise, for many centuries China was ruled by kings, who were guided by sages, such as Kung Fu Tzu (Confucius), Lao Tzu and Chuang Tzu in the BC era. Even later, Chinese monks played a very important role in leadership by guiding the rulers through *parables*, where they used to grant wisdom to the rulers without blaming but making clear to them the consequences of their brutal actions.

The Muslim world had their golden time during Caliphate—spiritual governance based on justice and kindness—which ended with the fall of Ottoman Empire. In India, during the Mughal period, Akbar had appointed *nava ratana*s (nine jewels—nine wise men)—people of wisdom and sagacity as king's advisors.

Indian sages are known for their sagacity. Many rulers used to appoint sages and monks as their advisors. Chanakya was an Indian philosopher and royal advisor to Maurya Empire during 300 BC. The names of many Indian *sant*s (saints), sages and Sufis can be quoted whose sagacity provided heart to Indian politics. The names of Tulsidas, Baba Farid, Kabir Das, Jeevan Das Dadu (disciple of Kabir), Sant Tukaram, Guru Nanak, Hazarat Nizamuddin, Muinuddin Chishti, Amir Khusro can be quoted whose sagacity created impact on local politics. Their teachings through poetry or lectures were highly respected by people and considered worthy of healing the wounds of mankind by purifying the society.

Besides India are Iran, Afghanistan, Syria, Iraq, Lebanon—the lands with spiritual fertility—where Sufism flourished. To name a few: Kahlil Gibran, Jalal el-Din Rumi, Omar Khyyam, Al Arabi, Shirazi, Mansur al-Hallj, Hafiz, Al-Ghazali, Rabiah of Basra, Bibi Jamal Khatun.

In olden Greece, sages like Socrates, Heraclitus, Plato and Aristotle played important roles in the ancient politics by guiding the rulers through their philosophy and sagacity. Socrates preferred to drink Hemlock but never defied people. Aristotle was the spiritual guru of Alexander the Great. Today, the same Athens has economically collapsed when people turned to lust and greed with the materialistic outlook.

Among Sufis of the modern era, Kahlil Gibran (1883–1931) stands tall. His sagacity was so versatile that guided mankind on

> **Enlargement**
>
> When you long for blessings that you may not name, and when you grieve knowing not the cause, then indeed you are growing with all things that grow, and rising towards your greater self.
>
> —Kahlil Gibran, *The Greatest Works of Kahlil Gibran*

every aspect of life, including leadership. No wonder, his famous work *The Prophet* has been included in curricula as reference book for MBA students by many institutes, including XLRI, Jamshedpur. He finds lion's share in this book for his versatility as well as relevance of his sagacity to modern times.

Kahlil Gibran possessed a loving heart of a Sufi, where hatred found no place. His great work was highly inspirational for developing the true leadership traits. He respected all the religions of the world and stood for bringing about unity. Today's world as well as corporate world needs leaders with Sufi Sagacity to heal the wounds of mankind and infuse soul into the soulless business houses. More than technology, which is spiritually empty, rather bank corrupt, sagacity in leadership is the need of the day.

Where are these sages in today's world? I am not suggesting that sages must rule the world; what I am suggesting is that today's leaders must benchmark with ancient sages and acquire Sufi Sagacity in leadership, both in corporate and political spheres. They must grow above racial and religious prejudices. The political system as well as commercial organisations must undergo a drastic change.

Today we use brilliance for strategies formation keeping focus on business success, by hook or by crook. Many a time in anxiety to make money we formulate crooked business strategies and go astray. If you develop a Sufi Heart, it will never allow cheating the man in the mirror. 'Sell your cleverness and buy bewilderment'[3] is the Sufi advice that comes from a great Sufi, Rumi. It is better to quit than live in shame. It is better to fail than get success through treachery. *Treachery always commits suicide in long run.*

---

[3] Jelaluddin Rumi, *RUMI Daylight—A Daybook of Spiritual Guidance.*

A Sufi Heart beats for everyone, without making a distinction between a man and man on the basis of religion, region, nationality, caste, race or language.

Sufi Sagacity is the guiding force for *Leading Dil Se*. Today, world as well as corporate world need leaders who should lead with Sufi Sagacity! We need more *wisdom* than *knowledge*.

The nation of Love has a different religion of all religions—for lovers, God alone is the religion.

—Rumi

2

LEADERSHIP WITH SECULAR APPROACH

You are my brother and I love you. I love you when you prostrate yourself
in your mosque, and kneel in your church and pray in your synagogue.
You and I are sons of one faith—The Spirit.
—KAHLIL GIBRAN, *THE GREATEST WORKS OF KAHLIL GIBRAN*

M any countries do not have a role model of great leadership. India and Indian are lucky that we have a role model of a great leader—Mahatma Gandhi—who was highly secular in his thought and actions.

Mahatma Gandhi was one of the most secular leaders of world. Among many leadership traits, *secularity* predominated his leadership. In a plural society, secularity becomes the predominant characteristic of leadership. His greatness, inter alia, lied in his secular approach. His famous worship prayer was simple and highly secular: *Ishwar, Allah Tero Naam, Sab Ko Sanmati De Bhagwan*, meaning, 'Your names are Ishwar and Allah; Give Wisdom to all, O God'.

To my mind, M.K. Gandhi was more a Sufi than a politician. He was a saint than a statesman. He was more a mystic than a maven. That's why he is known as Mahatma—the Great Soul! He grew with a secular thought: 'God has no religion'.

Mahatma Gandhi was a brilliant student of many religions. Besides his profound study of Hinduism, Buddhism and Jainism, he had profoundly studied Islam and Christianity. This holistic understanding of man's spiritual quest led Gandhi to adopt and preach a theory of tolerance and mutual respect founded on truth and non-violence. He believed God is one and he variously equated Him to love and truth. For him, leading a godly life was more important than debating about true nature of God. The poor and the downtrodden were for Gandhi the living representatives of God on earth.

Mahatma Gandhi preached his ideals of secularism and religious tolerance across the length and breadth of the country. What he preached, he practiced and demonstrated in action.

Secular Perspective

If I were a dictator, religion and state would be separate. I swear by my religion. I will die for it. But it is my personal affair. The state has nothing to do with it. The state would look after your secular welfare, health, communications, foreign relations, currency and so on, but not your or my religion. That is everybody's personal concern.
—Mahatma Gandhi

Though Mahatma Gandhi and Pandit Nehru had differences on some issues, but they had strong mutual synergy on the vital issue of secularism. No wonder secularism has become the foundation of Free India. Among the developing countries, India is distinguished by its proclaimed commitment to secularism as the guiding principle state policy and leadership train. Many leaders from different religions made sacrifices in the pursuit of the secular ideal. Mahatma Gandhi with the death-defying courage and support of Jawaharlal Nehru could turn the dream into a reality.

To my mind, *secular approach* is the first and foremost important prerequisite trait in leadership, especially in today's world where religious intolerance, amidst the empty sermons for *religious tolerance* on every lip, has reached to the level of religious hatred. Corporate world, being the small segment of the same big world, is no more different. The only difference between these two *macro* and *micro* worlds is that in the former, this hatred is expressed overtly by a vocal section of public and diplomatically and guardedly by the governments, and in the latter the abhorrence and intolerance is not openly seen as it is delicately covered but strategically expressed in actions. There are many exceptions to such prejudices, but exceptions do not form a real pattern.

What does this word *secular* stands for?

If you go with its dictionary meaning, it stands for *worldly, non-spiritual, materialist, and irreligious approach.* Do we need this secular approach in politics or business? No, not at all! We look for approach diagonally apposite to the dictionary meaning of the word *secular.* When I say *secular approach,* I mean an unbiased, judicious and indiscriminate approach beyond religious, racial, colour or creed or linguistic prejudices with the heart filled with love for all people of different faiths. With this meaning, I proceed. If the word *secular* cannot give this meaning, it is time to redefine this word so it may give the desired meaning, which we really mean while using this word *secular.*

If we go with the spirit (not meaning), secularism stands for a modern political and legal principle, which involves two basic tenets. The first is that people belonging to different faiths and sections of society are equal before the law and the constitution and government policies. The second requirement is that there should be no discrimination against anyone on the basis of religion or faith, nor should there be any room for the hegemony of one religion or majoritarian religious sentiment and aspirations.

To my mind, the word *secular* is not *non-spiritual*; rather, it is highly spiritual as it is used in Indian society. Indian society is not a *non-spiritual society*; Indian society is highly spiritual society. Indian society is not an *irreligious* society; Indian society is highly a multi-religious society. Indian society does not stand in absence of God; Indian society stands with the presence of God. In Indian society, the word *secular* stands with a most positive connotation—a perfect spiritual understanding of various faiths with utmost respect to each faith, nor simply *tolerance*. When you base *secularism* on *tolerance*, you should not surprise when tolerance gives way to *intolerance*. The word *tolerance* is not a positive word, though it seems to be so as an opposite word to *intolerance*.

A secular leader must behave like a flowing river. 'We all get water from the river to quench our thirst,' believes an Indian Sufi Khwaja Moinuddin Chishti, 'It does not discriminate whether we are a relation or a stranger.' He further says,

> *He must display the hospitality like the Earth. We are raised and cradled in its lap, and yet it is always under our feet. He must have affection like the Sun. When the sun rises, it is beneficial to all irrespective of whether they are Muslim, Christian, or Hindu.*

The leaders must learn from the sun and serve their people indiscriminately.

Ethnic Harmony

Without respect for people of different races or ethnicities or religions, how can we have a peaceful and harmonious society, how can there be the necessary economic development and atmosphere conductive to spiritual happiness and self-realization?

—Jagad Guru

For real secular approach, the realm of validity of religion in the public arena and society should be necessarily limited. In personal life, religion must find utmost highest position; in social life, it should appear as one of the pleasant colours, which form beautiful pattern on the canvas. All religious places—temples, churches, gurudwaras and mosques—should be considered as the sacred places of worship for the particular people of that faith. If one disrespects other's place of worship, as consequence, others will disrespect one's place of worship. We live in consequences! We must understand this fact clearly.

A true leader is one who does not see a person through the colourful glasses, where people look different owing to their personal faith. Jalal ed-Din Rumi of Persia of 13th century guides the mankind through his Sufi poetry: 'Christian, Jew, Muslim, Shaman, Zoroastrian, stone, ground, mountain, river, each has a secret way of being with the mystery, unique and not to be judged.' Non-judgemental approach is akin to both, Sufism and secularism.

Despite the negative dictionary meaning and many weaknesses in actual practice, *secular approach* is most accepted style of leadership, both in politics and business. Those who spread hatred and abhorrence are becoming untouchables, both in society and business houses. What gives you success in short term does not provide sustainability. One may quote the examples of many leaders who appeared and disappeared like the water bubbles, despite their service to a section of society.

Plurality is not weakness but strength. A multicolour picture looks more appealing than a single colour pattern. The real synergy comes from diversity rather than from uniformity. Living in a plural society warrants more

> **Human Beings Are Inter-beings**
>
> If we have no peace, it is because we have forgotten that we belong to each other.
> —Mother Teresa

wisdom, values and, above all, mutual respect (not simply tolerance) than living in a single-religion political state. A new pattern emerges from different patterns. The differing faith and practices create a vivid pattern. Society becomes rich with the richness of various civilisations and cultures. Yet, the faith remains intact and unpolluted in the hearts of the respective followers. Let there be a clear understanding: 'I do not worship what you worship. You do not worship what I worship. You have your religion and I have

mine'.[1] Such understanding will help cultivate harmony and mutual respect for each other's faith and practices.

We are more spiritual beings rather than simply human beings.
We are more inter-beings rather than simply individual beings.
We live life with interdependence—without others we cannot survive. When it is clear to us that we cannot exist without others,
then we have only two options—live in peace and harmony loving
each other or live in chaos and disharmony hating each other.
Which is better?

Secular approach of leader is very important to defeat the prejudices. Amidst evil, the truth must prevail. Kahlil Gibran's sup-
plication, though strange but very meaningful: 'I have no enemies,
O God, but if I am to have an enemy, let his strength be equal
to mine, that Truth alone may be the victor!' How many leaders
of modern age dare ask God to test truth in their thoughts, approach and actions? We always defend our actions, even when our
conscience whispers to us otherwise. 'Perhaps a man may commit
suicide, in self-defense,' says Gibran.[2]

We judge people vis-à-vis our personal logic, stereotypes where
racial mind plays the vital role. We judge a person with the im-
pression that he creates in our mind. This is a very common practice; none finds anything wrong. Strange! Here is the Sufi message: 'You cannot judge any man beyond your knowledge of him,
and how small is your knowledge!'.[3]

In plural society, oppression of strong over weak is a very
common practice. It happens everywhere—it has been happening for eons. Kahlil Gibran's heart is sensitive to such dominance
and subjugation. He expects this sensitivity from the leaders who
would provide solace and heal the wounded souls through his
words and actions:

> I love you because you are weak before the strong oppressor, and poor before the
> greedy rich. For these reasons I shed tears and comfort you. And from behind

[1] The Holy Qur'an—109: 2–4 and 6.
[2] Kahlil Gibran, The Greatest Works of Kahlil Gibran.
[3] Ibid.

my tears I see you embraced in the arms of justice, smiling and forgiving your persecutors. You are my brother and I love you ... I love you, my brother, whoever you are—whether you worship in your church, kneel in your temple, or pray in your mosque. You and I are all children of one faith, for the diverse paths of religion are fingers of the loving hand of ONE Supreme Being, a hand extended to all, offering completeness of spirit to all, eager to embrace all.[4]

> **Bonding**
>
> Love and compassions are necessities, not luxuries. Without them, humanity cannot survive!
> —Dalai Lama, *The Path to Tranquility: Daily Meditations*

Can leaders of modern age develop a Sufi heart that beats for the entire mankind!

The entire mankind is the progeny of one father, call him Adam, Aadam or Manu. If one kills others, he kills his own brother. 'Is it honour for a man to kill his brother man?' asks Kahlil Gibran. 'If you deem it an honour, let it be an act of worship, and erect a temple to Cain, who slew his brother Abel'.[5] And if you feel you cannot build Cain's temple, you have got to believe that killing others cannot be an honour, it is ghastly crime, as ghastly as killing one's own brother.

The United Nations has emerged as one Great Nation to protect the interest of mankind. Many may not believe that the entrance hall of United Nations building in New York is graced with the Sufi couplet:

Of one Essence is the human race;
Thusly, had Creation put the Base;
One limb impacted is sufficient,
For all others to feel the Mace![6]

These beautiful couplets, which call for breaking all human barriers, were composed by Sufi of Sheraz of Persia, whose name

[4] Kahlil Gibran, *The Greatest Works of Kahlil Gibran.*
[5] Ibid.
[6] Sheikh Saadi Shirazi, *The Bostan of Saadi.*

was Sheikh Saadi. He is also known as Saadi Sherazi. He travelled all over the Middle East to understand and comprehend the riches of multi-culture, multi-civilisation political systems. He is considered one of the greatest Sufis of world who granted wisdom to mankind through his Sufi thoughts during the 12th century. He died yet survived through his Sufi spirit. I am happy that the Sufi thoughts find a conspicuous place at the entrance of the UN building, but my heart bleeds because the Sufi spirit does not dwell there anymore. The building, which was meant for souls to dwell, is occupied by bodies and minds, dominated by political interests rather than spiritual wisdom!

A leader with a Sufi heart would fight for truth protecting the innocent, staying above caste, creed or religious faiths. He would hate the sin not the sinner. His entire endeavour would be to correct rather than punish people.

If you wish to grow into a true leader for the good cause of mankind, rising above the personal prejudices is not enough. You must tune your ears not to get intoxicated with praise and pleasant words of the schemers. You must also train your ears not to hear the whispers of the gossipmongers, who always pollute the society with their exaggerated narrations of fact, sprinkling spices.

Seven centuries ago seven white doves rose from a deep valley flying to the snow-white summit of the mountain. One of the seven men who watched the flight said, 'I see a black spot on the wing of the seventh dove.'

Today the people in that valley tell of seven black doves that flew to the summit of the snowy mountain![7]

It does not take much time for miscommunication of a factual incident. When someone says I have seen a kite flying, next day people of the village will be telling a story of a flying saucer seen by someone.

Communication of truth is important. When you do not communicate the truth, the vacuum created by non-communication is

[7] Kahlil Gibran, *The Greatest Works of Kahlil Gibran.*

filled with grapevine and gossips and conjectures. Thus, not only truth must be communicated constantly but its effectiveness must also be ensured through proper feedback.

We have created many doctrines, which divide us despite their truthfulness. 'Many a doctrine is like a window pane. We see truth through it but it divides us from truth.' Likewise, each religion is sacred filled with truth, but it divides the mankind. If one cares to study beneath many ghastly bloodsheds, you will find the difference of ideologies in terms of faith, caste, creed, race, region or language as the root cause. A leader who is not capable to be above all these biases and prejudices will be incapable of protecting the differing faith and interests of mankind. How can he be taken or accepted as a leader in a pluralistic society?

Truth is always hazy at both ends. For this reason, it is difficult to see it. Then, devil—the archenemy of Man—always works against truth and never allows man to grasp it. Paulo Coelho, the author of famous book, *The Alchemist*, explains how Satan corrupts our nature and how sometimes human beings themselves corrupt truth by dividing it and giving it many names and shapes:

The devil was talking to his friends when they noticed a man who reached down to pick up something from the floor.

'Man found a piece of truth,' said the devil. His friends were very concerned. A piece or truth could save the soul of man and meant one less person in Hell. But the devil remained undisturbed, looking at the landscape.

'Do not worry', said the devil to his friends. 'Do you know what he will do with this piece? As always, he will create a new sect. And be able to move more people away from the whole truth.'*[8]

Truth Is Indivisible

The truth was a mirror in the hands of God. It fell and broke into pieces. Everybody took a piece of it, and they looked at it and thought they had the truth.

— Jelaluddin Rumi, *RUMI Daylight—A Daybook of Spiritual Guidance*

[8] Paulo Coelho, *Deccan Chronicle*.

Many books, which are written to teach us the truth, often take us away from the truth. This way truth loses its shape like the hat, which everyone tries to wear. As mentioned, *truth* is like seeing through a piece of glass; you can see the truth through it. But simultaneously the same piece of glass separates you from the truth, as it exists between you and the truth.

'Should you sit upon a cloud you would not see the boundary line between one country and another, nor the boundary stone between a farm and a farm. It is a pity you cannot sit upon a cloud'.[9] The great wisdom of Kahlil Gibran removes the mental barriers that we create on the basis of tribe, race and faith. When one rides the clouds, such barriers vanish. If we wish to lead a nation or a business house of tomorrow, you must acquire the skill and competence for riding the clouds, not sometimes, always.

A leader with a Sufi heart is highly secular who sits upon a cloud and sees no boundary lines that divide the mankind.

[9] Kahlil Gibran, *The Greatest Works of Kahlil Gibran*.

Trust thyself, *and another shall not betray thee!*
— *Benjamin Franklin*

3

Leadership Consciousness: Know Thyself

'Who am I?' is a difficult question to answer. Knowing 'thy self' is difficult. Ask the following questions and you see that the door to discovery of self opens slowly.

Am I the Body?
Am I the Mind?
Am I the Heart?
Am I the Soul?
Or
Am I the Cosmic whole?

Now ponder upon another vital question: *Whether I am a particle of dust in the cosmos or the entire cosmos is within me?*

Our body is made of cells. The cells are made of atoms. Science says that 99.999 per cent vacancy of each item is filled with energy. Then, *are we more energy OR matter? Are we more soul OR body?*

These are very subtle questions, which open the doors of enlightenment.

Now let us turn to business management.

Why do we call human beings as resource? Money, Material, Machines are resources for they are soul-less articles of trade. The human resource (HR) is not a right connotation. How can we equate man—who possesses soul—with dead things like money, material and machine, which do not have a soul? The terminology *Human Capital* is far more frustrating—a disgrace to the entire mankind. How long shall we ape the West? Human is a potential—a reservoir of energies.

I explain some basic issues before taking you to greater heights.

Man is an embodiment of many forms of energies. We may divide these energies in the following four groups:

1. Physical energy—Body
2. Mental Energy—Mind or Intellect
3. Emotional Energy—Heart
4. Spiritual Energy—Soul

Though each type of energy has a locale, yet they cannot be compartmentalised. They are not only all-pervasive but also have some connectivity with the cosmic energies; I call it *Cosmic Soul.*

Against this backdrop, let me try to give some pattern to human energies, which is only depictive (Figure 3.1). I am aware that energies cannot be given a physical pattern. The invisible remains invisible!

You do not need a leader to manage Human Capital. If *Human* is *Capital*, we know, capital is managed, not led. Likewise, you do not need a leader to manage HR. If *human* is *resource*, we know, resource is managed, not led. Soul-less is managed; soul-full is led.

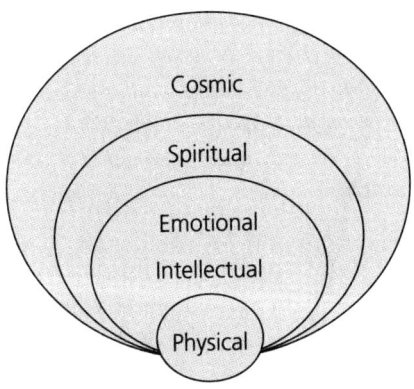

FIGURE 3.1
Human Energies

Source: This figure is the intellectual property of author's
consulting company Intellects Biz.

Human beings have soul, which can be spirited and inspired. For this, we need a leader, who has potential to harness the human potentials. Neither *Human Capital* nor *Human Resource* is a right connotation.

A leader must understand his people. But before understanding his people, he should understand himself. Understanding self and others is not easy.

'Only once have I been made mute when someone asked me, "Who are you?"' says Kahlil Gibran, a great Sufi of Lebanon.[1] It is not easy to understand one's own self. Many prophets, saints, philosophers and spiritual scientists devoted their lifetime to understand the self. Buddha is one among the multitude who devoted his whole life to understand the purpose of Man's existence on earth.

Osho, whose mystic thoughts were hailed by people of the East and West during the second half of 20th century, says that we do not know our own selves, as we never think about our inner self. What others say about us, we become so.

[1] Kahlil Gibran, *The Greatest Works of Kahlil Gibran.*

Right now, whatsoever you know about yourself is via other. Somebody says you are very nice and you believe it. Somebody says you are very intelligent and you believe it. One person says one thing, another person says another thing! You don't know anything about yourself directly. You know your face through a mirror, but a mirror can only reflect your mask. For the original face you have to go inward. You have to discover it at the very core of your being.[2]

Our real being is our inmost core; it is not somewhere outside. Osho considers soul as light and body as darkness. 'The body consists of darkness and the soul consists of light, and where this darkness and light meet, that is the territory of the mind. So mind has both—a little bit of light and light bit of darkness.' Mind is always restless, he believes.

Mind always remains in tension because it is being pulled in two opposite directions (by body and soul). Sometimes it chooses the body, sometimes it chooses the soul. But whatsoever it chooses there is always the feeling that it is wrong because the other has been left…. Mind means 'No Peace'; 'No Mind' means 'Peace'.[3]

As per Osho, 'mindlessness' renders peace.

Human consciousness expands as well as contracts. Likewise, leadership consciousness also expands and contracts as per changing perspective and level or understanding. As sometime wisdom comes as a sudden flash of light, leaders also get a sudden awakening and jump to the highest level of leadership consciousness without passing through various stages. Leaders are human beings; what applies to men applies to them. If man can become Buddha, leaders can also become Buddha. I place 'Sufi Sagacity' at the highest level of leadership-consciousness where consciousness-expansion maximises (Figure 3.2).

A leader, who does not recognise his soul is a leader whose heart is spiritually empty. When leaders grow heartless, unaware

---

[2] Osho, *The Inner Journey.*
[3] Ibid.

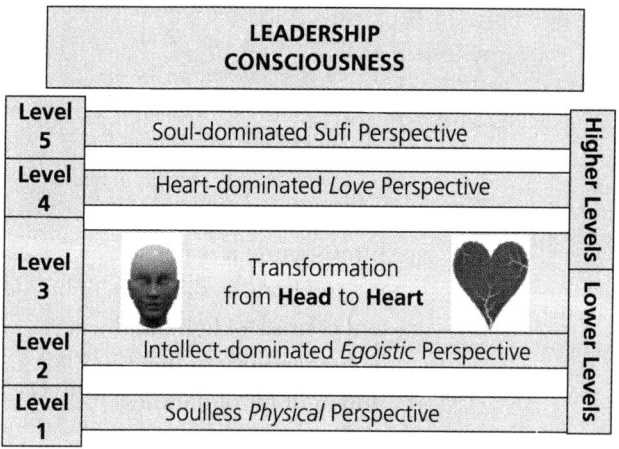

FIGURE 3.2
Leadership Consciousness

Source: This figure is the intellectual property of author's
consulting company Intellects Biz.

of the existence of soul, they get a skewed growth with lopsided approach. Such leaders lead from the lower levels of leadership-consciousness, with physical or egoistic perspective. A leader who cannot understand his real self, how can he understand the people whom he leads? A person, who cannot understand self, cannot understand others. Such (mis)leaders operate from the level of contracted consciousness.

Strange, we do not understand our real self! Although Man does not belong to the everlasting sphere of life, yet he is fated to live forever. On this earth he is perishable, but death does not put an end to his existence. Though his body is inferior and earthly, yet his spirit is lofty and everlasting. So, understand thyself, understand thy spirit—soul. Spirit exists in each of us by the command of the Supreme Being.

Those who recognise their soul understand thyself. They believe in the Hour of Judgement. They know they are answerable to the Supreme Being for their deeds, good or bad.

They understand the life reality and turn sober. They understand the Sufi Sagacity and develop a Sufi heart. They lead from the higher levels of leadership consciousness.

Between the two sets of lower levels and higher levels lies the phase of transformation—movement from head to heart. This is an important subject and therefore I have allotted a full chapter on this theme.

> **Grow beyond Five Sensory Perceptions**
>
> Just as ears cannot take cognisance of colour, nor the eye of sound, so, in conceiving the ultimate realities (God and Soul), we find ourselves in a region in which sense-concepts can bear no part.
>
> —Al-Ghazali, *The Alchemy of Happiness*

'He who knows himself knows God,' is a traditional saying of Prophet Mohammad. Almost all Sufis, saints and mystic masters believe that to understand God, first understand your *self*. 'Knowledge of "Self" is the gateway to happiness,' believes Al-Ghazali.[4] According to him there are four constituents for a wholesome discovery: (a) the knowledge of Self; (b) the knowledge of the Almighty God; (c) the knowledge of this Temporal World; and (d) the knowledge of the next Eternal World. To understand God, one has got to reach Him through Soul. 'The knowledge of Soul plays a most important part in leading to the knowledge of God than the knowledge of our body and the functions,' believes Ghazali. 'If a man knows not his own soul, how can he claim to know others?' asks the Sufi. Those who claim knowledge of others without understanding self are like a beggar 'who has not a wherewithal for a meal should claim to be able to feed the town'.[5]

You cannot understand *Thyself* through your five sensory perceptions. Your five sensory perceptions will not allow you to move from lower levels to higher levels of leadership-consciousness. Once you cross the barrier of five sensory perceptions, you

[4] Al-Ghazali, *The Alchemy of Happiness*.
[5] Ibid.

become a multi-sensory personality that takes you to higher levels of leadership-consciousness and you start leading *Dil Se*, employing Sufi Sagacity.

Human soul is pure. It is we who make it impure and corrupt by our evil deeds. Human soul contains in itself a constant conflict between good and evil. It is for you to instil in it *wickedness* or *God consciousness*. Each of us has a measure of goodness and a measure of evilness. Soul has the magnetic power to seek goodness and avoid evil. It always whispers to us, tells us to do something good to keep the soul healthy and pure. Yet, we are attracted to the whispers of the Devil who invites and incites us to commit sins and misdeeds. The one who keeps his soul healthy and purifies it by good deeds succeeds in this world and hereafter—the eternal life. He is the person who can lead from higher levels of leadership-consciousness.

Many political leaders and corporate managers grow in politics and business without recognising their souls. They grow heartless. Those who do not recognise their soul, in fact, deny recognising *Thyself*. As man cannot smell through tongue nor taste with nose, a man cannot recognise his soul through five sensory perceptions. Soulless leaders cannot rise beyond the two lower levels of leadership-consciousness.

When I say recognise your soul, I mean believe that you have a soul. This much understanding is sufficient because it is difficult to explain, 'what is Spirit or Soul?' It is not wise to describe that which cannot be described. There are certain things in life that even saints do not know or understand.

> **Acquire Spiritual Knowledge**
>
> A person in whom the desire for 'Spiritual Knowledge' has disappeared is like one who has lost his appetite for healthy food.
> —Al-Ghazali, *The Alchemy of Happiness*

Too much enquiry into certain aspects, which are beyond the capacity of human understanding, lets one go astray. We try to explain everything without realising that we are leading people astray. Spirit or soul is one such thing, which cannot be explained. Human mind is not mature enough to understand or comprehend the spirit. So, it is wiser to become intuitive and believe in certain aspects of life, which cannot be understood or explained through logic. *Logic* is a little infant before the *intuitive giant*. So, you must trust your intuitive wisdom to recognise your soul—logic cannot take you to the higher levels of consciousness.

In the same breath, let me hasten to add that all that I have just said does not mean that one should shy away from finding the truth. Pursuance of knowledge is the alchemy to happiness. Both, internal and external knowledge are good for the health of *heart* and *head*.

We must develop an inquisitive mind and train it to ponder upon these softer aspects of life. Reflection gets you the deeper understanding. When you reflect through your heart, it opens the gates of infinite truth. 'Reflections is the lamp of the heart,' says Imam Al-Haddad, 'If it departs, the heart will have no light.'

Sometimes it so happens that we understand the truth but are not able to explain it constructively through the use of language. Language is finite. Sometimes it fails to explain even the finite. Then, how can the *finite* explain the *infinite*? Your body is finite but your soul is infinite. The law of the Lord, therefore, forbids too close an enquiry into the essence of spirit.

Many manage from the lower levels of leadership-consciousness and disappear like the water bubbles. Only those who move to higher levels of consciousness, leave behind them their footprints on the sands of time for the guidance of mankind. *Leading Dil Se* with Sufi Sagacity is leading from higher levels of leadership-consciousness—lower levels find no place in this book.

Sell your Cleverness *and buy* Bewilderment!

—*Rumi*

4

JOURNEY FROM 'HEAD' TO 'HEART'

If you cannot work with love but only with distaste it is better that you should leave your work and sit at the gate of the temple and take alms of those who work with joy!
—KAHLIL GIBRAN, *THE GREATEST WORKS OF KAHLIL GIBRAN*

The change from *head* to *heart* does not happen instantly, but some stark reality becomes the turning point. Yet it takes time to grow in wisdom—it takes time to move from *head* to *heart*. Let me begin with a 'Moment of Truth' that became a turning point in my life:

'What happened to my demand I made the other day?' Moolanaganna, a very notorious union leader from one of my factories stopped me in the corridor, finding me alone. A few of his musclemen followed him demonstrating their loyalty for him. It was midnight. I was coming out from the conference hall after long negotiations on wage revision of HMT, which had failed. I was quite tired and also disappointed as a management we had failed in settling the issue amicably on the negotiation table. My chairman and directors had already left but many union leaders were still wandering here and there in batches. I didn't even remember the issue Moonlanaganna was referring to. So, I politely told him that it was not time to discuss IR issues in the corridor dead at night. But he was bent upon to create a scene.

'Whether you will do it or not. I want your answer in YES or NO,' he commanded.

As mentioned, I was not in good mood, so I told him, 'When I do not even remember your demand, how can I promise or give any assurance?' I wanted to move but his followers stopped me. Moolanaganna shouted, 'Say, Yes or No.' They were trying to terrorise me.

I made up my mind to face them strongly. I said 'No', raising the pitch of my voice. Upon this he shouted, 'I will kill you, right now.' His companions also moved closer to terrorise me. I am used to such situations and knew how to handle them. But, as I mentioned, I was dejected and tired, I lost my cool and started shouting upon him using many filmy dialogue, 'Agar Maan Ka Doodh Pia Hai To Aa and Maar!' *(If you have sucked the milk of your mother come and kill me). My voice was so loud and wild that it echoed in the huge palatial building. Some other union leaders from corporate office heard me and came running to stop the scuffle. A few of them were my supporters. They scolded Moolanaganna and his stooges. He and his fellows had to eat the humble pie. I emerged as a champion.*

The next morning my HR colleagues from different factories started sending their compliments for having demonstrated guts and taking the bull by horn. When I was climbing the mountain of pride receiving good feed for my ego, the personal secretary of Mr PC Neogy, my Chairman and Managing Director, told that CMD wanted to see me immediately. I went to him.

'Siddiqui, can you narrate what had happened yesterday night after other directors and I left?' I verbatim narrated the entire episode, including my Hindi filmy dialogues, expecting a hug or pat from my boss.

'I never expected this from "My Siddiqui",' he told with a gentle smile. I felt as if I had fallen from the heights. I was not only unhappy but also disappointed. He could read my face and understood my hurt feelings. His words of solace came to me.

'Siddiqui, tell me honestly, did you lose your "cool" strategically or "emotionally"?' *he asked.*

'Sir, I had lost my cool and shouted on them using the words came to my tongue in anger.' I replied expressing my anguish and disappointment.

'Then,' he told after a pause, 'Siddiqui, you get a ZERO mark.' I didn't ask 'Why'. I was highly disgusted and disappointed getting a sermon instead

of praise. Mr Neogy remained patient. He then gave a big bhashan *(lecture) on* krodh *(anger) and* akrodh *(negation of anger). 'You cannot counter* krodh *with* krodh,' *he said. '*Krodh *can only be countered with* akrodh. *Moolnaganna made a mistake and you made another mistake. Can two mistakes make one right action?" he asked. Then he gave me the example of Jesus Christ's sermon of offering another cheek and Buddha's philosophy. 'You cannot counter hatred with hatred; hatred can be countered only with love.' His sermon was good but I was not able to take it, as I was not in a receptive mood.*

Years passed by. But I could not forget Mr Neogy's sermon. Though I did not like it at that moment, but later, as I started thinking, it made a lot of sense to me. Yes, he was right.

Later, when I read the life and thoughts of many Sufis and saints, prophets and messengers of God, my arrogance succumbed to my humility. Believe it or not, Mr Neogy's sermon was the turning point in my life. Gradually I started moving from *head* to *heart*.

When I say turning point, it was not that I had seen some divine glow. Nor did I see white pigeons or angel descending from the sky. Neither did I hear any divine music, nor see the bright light flashes. What I did notice was a strange change inside me. I was aware now more than ever before that it was time to shift from *egotism* to *altruism*—from *egoistic* perspective to *love* perspective. The journey is not over; I am still struggling while inching ahead.

The journey of great distance that only a few have dared to travel is the journey from Head to Heart. In my case it is only a beginning. I have not travelled the full distance; I am still on my way travelling a great distance. While proceeding ahead with my heart, my mind tries to pull me back. My intellect challenges my intuitive wisdom

> **Life Secret**
>
> To your mind feed *understanding*;
> To your heart, *tolerance* and *compassion.*
> The simpler your life, the more meaningful!
> The less you desire of the world,
> The more room you will have in it
> To fill with the Beloved.
> —Shaikh Abu-Saeed Abil-Kheir, *Nobody Son of Nobody*

and creates noise cautioning me to be 'beware of heart'—the deceiver. But I have started trusting my heart over my mind. I love my heart. I love my emotions. But it is not that I do not consult my mind. Sometimes it goes with heart; sometimes it opposes. I keep the final choice with me. Anyhow, I am only a beginner. But I am not a lone traveller!

Your mind and heart play different roles—the first gets you intellects and the latter, wisdom. The mind gets you the riches of the world; the heart gets you the Heavenly Blessings. So, one must know the art of using one's mind and heart.

Why the journey from mind to heart is considered most difficult, tedious and longest? I will explain borrowing the Sufi insight from Osho, a mystic guru:

Mind is argumentative, it goes on arguing and arguing and infinitum. It keeps you engaged but it never gives you any conclusion. It is inconclusive—that is its nature. That is why philosophy has not been able to give a single conclusion to humanity. It has been an utter futile exercise and for thousands of years, thousands of most brilliant people have remained engaged in that stupid work. The mind argues but never reaches any conclusion; the heart argues never and knows the conduction. This is how it is—this is one of the mysteries of life. The mind is very noisy but all the noise is useless; the heart is silent but delivers the goods.[1]

Touch the Eternity

It is only the loving heart that can touch the heart of humanity. The mind is shallow and superficial. It knows nothing of the height and depths. The mind is idiotic, it is always mediocre. It cannot give you any insight into reality. For that your heart needs to function—and love is nothing but the humming of the heart.

—Osho, *The Inner Journey*

Therefore, 'move from the Head to the Heart', suggests Osho. 'Move from argument to non-argument and life suddenly becomes a new phenomenon, full of significance, beauty and fragrance, full of light and love. And all these combined together is the meaning of divinity'.[2]

[1] Osho, *The Inner Journey*.
[2] Ibid.

Yet leaders lead and managers manage without using their hearts.

Before putting our best foot forward, let us understand clearly that the road that leads from head to heart not paved with roses; it is a most tedious journey on the pathway with full of thorns. But, should it deter us? 'If you are irritated by every rub, how will your mirror be polished?' asked the great Sufi Rumi.[3]

Initially, for many centuries, the owners of factories and mines were interested only in the physical energy of each worker. Henry Ford's famous sentence makes it clear that just 100 years back, business leaders were only interested in the human body of their people: 'One of my biggest frustrations is that when I hire people, I hire them for their hands. The frustration is that I have to take the *whole person* to get them.'

The history of the corporate world is the history of exploitation of the *physical energies* of workers. They were hired only to use their hands, and not their brains, let alone the heart or soul. For hundreds of years, workers' physical energies were used in factories and mines. A few decades ago, management recognised the potential of the *mind* of the hired workers and started using their mental or *intellectual energies*. Today, we proudly use the terminologies *intellectual capital*, *knowledge workers*, *cyber workers*, etc.

During the early days of industrial society, the job of managers was to clip the feathers of the workers so that they could never think of flying. All strategies were formulated just to harness their physical energies and to discourage them using their mind power. It was not their job. How could workers think? Workers were taken as another form of slaves, who were hired for their physical labour and not for their mental abilities. If their wings were not clipped, some of them might fly and create problem for the management. This led to class struggle and later what is known as the 'Class War'.

Corporate pharaohs used and misused the physical potential of people for eons. For the last few decades, they have started

[3] Jelaluddin Rumi, *RUMI Daylight—A Daybook of Spiritual Guidance*.

Fly; Don't Crawl!

You were born with potential.
You were born with goodness and trust.
You were born with ideals and dreams.
You were born with greatness.
You were born with wings.
You are not meant for crawling, so don't.
You have wings.
Learn to use them and fly.
—Jelaluddin Rumi, *RUMI Daylight—A Daybook of Spiritual Guidance*

using intellectual potential of human assets. They talk of 'Emotional Intelligence', but believe me many do not even understand it. They are not even aware where these energies rest in human body—Emotions reside in the Heart and Intelligence in the Mind. Unless you join your Mind with the Heart, you cannot harness emotional intelligence. As regards spiritual energy not only corporate world but also the *world* per se is allergic to spiritual potential of human beings. Many do not believe in this energy. Those who believe are hesitant to talk loudly about it.

Why has not the corporate world harnessed the *spiritual energies* of people? This is because many corporate pharaohs do not trust the human soul; many do not recognise the existence of the human soul. Even the so-called new age corporate world is grossly harnessing the physical and intellectual potential, and to some extent, emotional potential of its people. Corporate world has not recognised and harnessed the *spiritual potential* of the people. Why did the human soul not get recognition from the corporate world? This is because most of the corporate pharaohs are *spiritually challenged*. Many of them suffer from *spiritual blindness*, as they cannot see beyond the five sensory perceptions. Their hearts are spiritually empty. Many do not even recognise the existence of a Supreme Being—God.

Soul dwells in the heart. Once the leaders or managers develop a Sufi heart, they create the dwelling place for their soul, where it can get nourished and nurtured to the greatest extent.

We surrender, as we do not realise our real potential. Discover self; discover others. The real leader not only understands his potential but also help the followers to discover their potential. Do not crawl, do not let your people crawl. Understand your potential and fly.

Trust your inner self; trust God. Trusting God begins with trusting your *inner self*. Once you start trusting your inner self, your intuitive faculties get sharpened. You get God through your intuitive wisdom. Logic is crude—it often fails in understanding the finer aspects of life. When you look inwards, you find the hidden treasures of your soul. It is the soul that recognises God.

Extrasensory Perception (ESP) is no more an illusion. Science has already recognised the extraordinary faculties of the human mind—which can take you beyond the five sensory perceptions. The scientists assign this ability to the power of the mind because they have not yet recognised the existence of the soul. They are *soul shy* creatures. If they recognise and accept the soul, they will lose their identity of being scientists. Both Isaac Newton and Albert Einstein had discovered more than what they gave to the world. They were apprehensive of losing their identity as scientists if they shared those discovered truths about the softer aspects of life.

For harnessing spiritual energies of your people, first recognise the existence of God and the human soul. For this, create a Sufi heart—the heart filled with love for God and His mankind.

They say, God favours a prepared mind; He bends the heavens to pave the way for making things happen. But it is heart that takes you there. A leader must know that a mission can be planned from mind but it cannot be completed unless he puts his heart there.

I repeat, I shall repeat it again and again till my tongue bleeds—the journey of greatest distance that only a few dare travel is the journey from *head* to *heart*. And travelling from political mind or strategic mind to a Sufi heart is far more difficult. It takes time to grow in wisdom.

If you wish to live life as life wishes you to live, let your love become unlimited! Your soul grows with love, and cruelty with hate and fear. To become a great leader, create a Sufi's loving heart where *fear* and *hate* find no place because the unlimited space of the heart is filled with unlimited *love*.

Learn to like *what you do*. Most of the time, we take pride in saying, 'I do what I like.' It is good that you do what you like. It is great if you like what you do! Life fills your heart with happiness when you start practising, 'I love what I do!'

If you put your heart in the work, your mind and body shall follow. Fill your heart with passion and then do your work.

It is better not to do a thing if you cannot put your heart there. You can put your heart only when you acquire passion for liking what you do. Martin Luther King Jr rightly says that if you are told to be a street sweeper, sweep the streets—just as Michelangelo painted or Beethoven composed music or Shakespeare wrote poetry. Sweep the streets so well that all the hosts of heaven and earth will praise you and say, 'Here lived a great street sweeper who did his job well.' Loving what you do is better than doing what you love.

A leader who sees all beings in his own self and his own self in all beings loses all fear and he will not hate others. Again, a leader who sees all beings in his own self and his own self in all beings gains love and compassion for others. There is a spiritual link between all beings. Once you recognise your soul within, you become a part of the whole.

Once someone asked Sheikh Saadi to explain the virtue of sword in statesmanship. He replied, 'Sword is of two kinds— sword of steel and sword of love. The steel sword divides ONE into TWO; the love sword unites TWO into ONE.' So, use the steel sword if you want to perish; use the love sword if you wish to prosper. Both the swords kill. The steel sword kills love and love sword kills hatred. Yet, choice remains with each of us.

If you want to grow a true leader, live your truest life, fill your heart with so much love and passion that there remains no place for hatred. For this you are required to undertake a great journey—a journey from your *head* to *heart*. 'Only from the Heart can you touch the sky,' believes Rumi—a great Sufi.[4]

The common DNA of all great leaders is: *They travelled from Head to Heart!* They lead from within.

[4] Jelaluddin Rumi, *RUMI Daylight—A Daybook of Spiritual Guidance.*

For ages you have come and gone
courting the delusion.
For ages you have run from the pain
and forfeited the ecstasy.
So come, return to the roots of the root
of your own Soul.

—*Rumi*

5

LEADING 'INSIDE-OUT'

Life is not worth living,
Without a purpose or meaning!

—BUDDHA

Alice, who was chasing Bunny, fell into the rabbit hole and when she got up she found herself in the Wonderland. After enjoying the wonderments, she got disgusted and wanted to return but she could not find the way to go out. While wandering she saw the Cheshire Cat, sitting on the branch of a tree, she thought of seeking his help. 'Which way I aught to go from here?' Alice asked. 'That depends a good deal on where you want to go to?' Cheshire Cat replied. Since Alice was frustrated, she told, 'I don't much care, Where!' Upon this, Cheshire Cat smiled and said, 'Then it doesn't matter, which way you go!'.[1]

'If you don't know where you are going?' says Buddha, 'Any road will take you there.' We must know our destination then only select the path. Many times we go on climbing the so-called ladder

[1] Lewis Carroll, *Alice's Adventures in Wonderland*.

of success only to discover later that the ladder was leaning to the wrong wall.

Leading to achieve a purpose is leading *inside-out*; leading heedlessly chasing the mirage is leading *outside-in*. Let me elaborate. In 'outside-in' approach, leader starts by taking all the external factors into account—the available skills and competencies of his people, and various resources; in short, the whole caboodle that makes an organisation thick. Then the leader hunkers down to the task of determining what can be feasibly achieved from the available resources. In this approach, the focus is on *resources*, and aspects like *meaning* and *purpose* are shoved into the background.

In the *inside-out* approach, the leader begins with a simple existentialistic question: 'Why do I exist' or 'Why does my organization exist?' He first tries to identify the meaning or purpose of life or the corporate life, and then finds the means to accomplish the purpose. After searching his soul once he discovers the purpose of being, he starts looking for the means to manage the external environment—tapping into resources, building networks and honing skills. The journey begins from *within*. If the purpose is profound and powerful, leader needs to exert very little. The power of purpose makes things happen.

Buddha, who was born in the 6th century BC, passionately believed that life had a meaning and a purpose. People could lead meaningful lives if they understood its underlying purpose. It is much the same with organisations or nations. Purpose is the driving force—both in personal and corporate lives. The political life is no different. A purposeless life is no life.

Inside-Out

If you don't seek meaning, no vision can drive you towards excellence.

—Ken Blanchard,
The Heart of a Leader

It is an ancient belief that each soul when incorporated into the body makes a promise to the Supreme Truth—a covenant—to pursue an agreed purpose in life. However, once it enters the temporal world, it is blinded and deflected from its purpose by material comforts, glamour, fame, greed, lust and the other enchantments of worldly life. The soul, which is imprisoned within the human core we call the *body*, turns it back on this agreed commitment. But once in a while, the soul whispers to the mind and the body and reminds them the committed promise. This creates perturbation that purports one to begin the search for meaning in life—and the quest harks back to the promise that the soul had made to God at the time of incarnation. It is this quest that had transformed Siddhartha to Buddha.

Leading *inside-out* is possible only when the leader has illuminated his heart and recognised his powerful inner self. When you start trusting your inner self, you grow spiritual and start leading from within. Everything that exists in the external world exists within. 'If Milky Way were not within me how should I have seen it or known it?' asks Kahlil Gibran, Sufi of Lebanon.[2]

Some leaders develop their inner self so strong that they can see the unseen and hear the unheard. I am not creating poetry by using some phonetic words; I am saying this because I have witnessed this happening.

During my Nagarjuna days, a strange incident occurred. After serving five premier public sector undertakings I moved to a private sector company as Executive Vice President—Human Potential Development. K.S. Raju was our Chairman and Managing Director. We used to call him KS.

Once KS took the top Nagarjuna team to one of the project sites where oil refinery was coming up. After a hectic meeting, we had dinner in the British times old building near the project site. It was buffet. I finished my dinner and took a bowl of ice cream. Somehow I was tempted to take another bowl, but a bit hesitant thinking in my heart what people would think about their HR Chief? I heard KS saying, 'Moid why are you hesitant—if you feel like taking another bowl of ice cream take it'. I looked at KS who was discussing with couple of people with his back to me. He did

---

[2] Kahlil Gibran, *The Greatest Works of Kahlil Gibran*.

not even turn. I was shockingly surprised—does he possess an extra pair of eyes on the back of his head! I just said, 'KS, how could you say so!' Then he turned to me and asked, 'Moid were you not hesitant for taking the second bowl of ice cream?' Seeing me astonished, everyone turned to me to find out was it a fact what KS told with his back to me. And I confirmed in affirmation. How can one explain this episode?

Management gurus say 'Lead from front'. I would say, *lead from within!* Do not copy anyone. Do not try to choose the defined patterns of leadership. Work on your inner self. Your leadership should be the reflection of your inner self—the true self. 'The true great man is he who would master no one, and who would be mastered by none,' says Kahlil Gibran.[3]

Jalal ed-Din Rumi, a great Persian Sufi, who, as per one survey in 2007, was described as the most popular ancient poet in America, was an advocate of *inner self*. Those who do not understand their inner strength are like wingless words who crawl rather than flying. 'You were born with wings, why prefer to crawl through life?'[4]

Don't Look Elsewhere

You wander from room to room
Hunting for the diamond necklace
That is already around your neck!

— Jelaluddin Rumi, *RUMI Daylight—A Daybook of Spiritual Guidance*

Today everyone seems to be running, but in fact it is worse than crawling. When you run heedlessly you go astray wasting your energies. Many busy entrepreneurs and CEOs are no different than Kabir's *musk deer*. Without any internal clarity, they are speeding up in a mad rush for gaining the competitive edge and finally burning themselves. As the stupid *musk deer*, they are running through the endless maze of sense-objects, building empires, earning, spending, acquiring, exploiting, wasting all and striving for

---

[3] Kahlil Gibran, *The Greatest Works of Kahlil Gibran*.
[4] Jelaluddin Rumi, *RUMI Daylight—A Daybook of Spiritual Guidance*.

more only to make themselves exhausted. They ultimately dry up out of their own exhaustion, without getting the joy and satisfaction they are seeking. It is time for leaders to reflect and introspect. Think in peace. Try to understand the rhythmic cosmic principles—the Laws of Energy Response, as the Old Master Lao Tzu calls them—with intellectual neatness and you will find yourself on a different plane, much higher than money and material gains.

Rumi, the Sufi of Persia, was recognised as the greatest Sufi of his time, who was in divine love with God. He always looked the truth within, rather than searching it outside. 'Remember, the entrance door to the sanctuary is inside you. We rarely hear the inward music, but we are all dancing to it, nevertheless. You think the shadow is substance'.[5] The Sufi heart always looks within and discovers the truth. Seeing the unseen and hearing the unheard is great Sufi virtue, which a leader must acquire.

Like Kahlil Gibran and many other Sufis, Rumi also believed in the power of inner self—truth lies within. The entire universe exists within you:

You are a volume in the divine book
A mirror to the power that created the universe
Whatever you want, ask it of yourself
Whatever you're looking for can only be found
Inside of you.[6]

Rumi believes that each human being has inner light, and he is aware of it. 'There is a candle in your heart, ready to be kindled. There is a void in your soul, ready to be filled. You feel it, don't you?' he asks. Everyone is aware of the power of inner self yet we don't explore. 'Everything in the universe is within you,' Rumi claims and suggests, 'Ask all from yourself.' One has to clean one's inner self constantly. 'Be like melting snow—wash yourself of yourself'.[7]

[5] Jelaluddin Rumi, *RUMI Daylight—A Daybook of Spiritual Guidance.*
[6] Ibid.
[7] Ibid.

We have exaggerated *materialism* and chosen materialistic approach much beyond it deserved. This way we have become 'Five Sensory Leader' who is blind to intuitive wisdom. Today we need and look for *multisensory* leadership with an intuitive eye. A true leader is one whose understanding is beyond five sensory perceptions. Only such leaders can lead *inside-out*.

> **Look Within**
>
> One night as I sat in quiet, I seemed on the verge of entering a world inside, so vast! I know it is the source of all of us.
>
> —Meera Bai

Seeing, hearing, smelling, touch-feeling and tasting are crude sensory perceptions that even animals possess. In fact, in these five sensory perceptions human beings cannot compete with animals. The eagle can see farthest. Insects can hear the weakest sound frequencies. Sniff dog can smell and recognise which human being cannot do. Even a blindfish can touch-feel and find its path. A mongoose can taste deadly snakes poison.

Human beings are different from animals owing to their interior, not exterior. Truth lies within our interior, not in exterior.

Coming back to Nagarjuna, once again let me narrate another episode about KS—a *multisensory leader*. *Multisensory leadership* is not a utopia. One morning we were discussing the changing *business character* where *business ideology* would call shots, pushing *business strategies* to the backseat. The values of the company should not change, but the business strategies can change, rather should change as per the changing pattern of business character. Whereas the former is *Core*, the latter is *Non-core*. A value-based company must continually remind itself of crucial distinction between *what should never change and what should be open to change*. The core values must form a rock-solid foundation and must not drift with the changing trends. While keeping the core ideology tightly fixed, the value-based companies must display a powerful drive for progress that enables them to change and adapt without compromising their cherished core ideology.

I began to share my thoughts, saying, 'A high profile, charismatic style is clearly not required for building the "business ideology". How well the organisation brings out the great energies and talents of its people with focus on its value system will determine the long-term growth and sustainable success. In a value-based company, the core values do not need any rational or supporting justification.' After a pause I added, 'Nor should the company shift its focus in response to changing marketing conditions.'

The thought process continued, as KS watched calmly. He is known for being an 'avid listener'. Many thoughts came about but somehow I had a feeling they were blurred and hazy, lacking clarity; everyone was simply beating about the bush! K.S. Raju got up and wrote a simple sentence on the white board: *Internal Clarity leads to External Solutions!* How true!

Internal clarity is the seed of *inside-out*. If you don't have clarity within, you cannot find the path—you cannot identify and locate the required resources. The *inside-out* leadership begins from inner self.

This incident reminds me of a great Sufi, Al-Ghazali. In his famous book *The Alchemy of Happiness*, Ghazali writes, 'Man's five senses are like five doors opening on external world; but, more wonderful than this, his heart has a window which opens the unseen world of spirits. His heart like a mirror reflects what is pictured in the "Tablet of Fate"'. Not only Ghazali, all Sufis believe that the inner self is much more powerful than outer self. 'The first step to "self knowledge" is to know that you are composed of an outward shape, called the body, and an inward entity called the heart or soul,' writes Ghazali, 'By heart I do not mean the piece of flesh situated in the left of our bodies but that which uses all the other faculties as its instruments and servants.' The knowledge that common people acquire by laborious learning comes to Sufis through their intuitive wisdom.

I am not sure whether KS (K.S. Raju) has read Kahlil Gibran, but his belief is akin to great Sufi's thoughts.

All things in this creation exist within you, and all things in you exist in creation. There is no border between you and the closest things, and there is no distance between you and the farthest things, and all things, from the lowest to the loftiest, from the smallest to the greatest, are within you as equal things. In one drop of water are found the secrets of all the endless oceans; in one aspect of you are found all the aspects of existence.

Thus, everything you see outside is within you.

Grow as a Multisensory Leader

How ignorant are those who see, without question, the abstract existence with some of their senses, but insist upon doubting until that existence reveal itself to all their senses. Is not the sense of the heart as truly as sight is the sense of the eye?

—Kahlil Gibran, *The Greatest Works of Kahlil Gibran*

One day something strange happened. KS did not come to office, as he was not feeling well. Rahul, his son, had some urgent issues so he insisted me to go along with him to the house and discuss it with KS. I never wanted to disturb KS, but decided to go with Rahul as he was insistent. When I reached their house and met KS, he was not well owing to high temperature. Yet, he greeted both of us. After discussing on business issues, he asked Rahul to go back to office and desired that I should stay with him for some time, as he has to discuss something with me privately. When Rahul left, he began, 'Moid, I am fully aware what is happening to you. Some top guys are creating problems for you, yet you are fighting strongly to protect values. I want to give you confidence—what you are doing is right and you will find my fullest support.'

He paused. Then, he took my hand in his hands. I found it was very warm. Obviously, he was having high temperature. After a long pause he told me, 'Moid, a time will come when I will turn my eyes against you and will go favouring your opponents. At that time you shall remind me of this day, and I will again resume my support to you.' I kept silent. I did not know why he was cautioning me of the day when he would withdraw from me his support! He could perhaps read my mind, yet did not offer clarification. He simply whispered, 'Moid don't forget reminding me of my promise to you.' I promised and left his house with a confused mind. After a few months I found my opponents became very powerful and they started playing mischief by adopting some mean tactics. I could see that KS was no more with me. As per my promise, I was supposed to remind him, but I chose not to do so and decided to leave the organisation with my head high.

There are certain things in life that one cannot explain. I do not know why did KS caution me and took my promise that I would remind him his promise to regain his support. One door was closed, but many doors opened for me. I have no regrets, but I could not resolve the mystery. Even after leaving Nagarjuna Group I met him many times but the mystery of KS's words remained a mystery! One thing I can say for KS—his inner self is very strong. I learnt many things from him.

We trust our body, our mind, but do not trust our heart and soul. We try to understand everything, tangible and intangible, through our five sensory perceptions. Alas! We believe in logic and reasoning and trust not our intuitive wisdom. The truth cannot be comprehended by logic and reasoning, even if you spend your lifetime. Guru Nanak, an Indian Sufi, explains this truth in simple words: 'One cannot comprehend Him through reason, even if one reasoned for ages.'

Those who do not know how to lead from within are like the fox that measures his stature by seeing his own shadow. 'A fox looked at his shadow at sunrise and said, "I will have a camel for lunch today." And all morning he went about looking for camels. But at noon he saw his shadow again—and he said, "A mouse will do."' How truly Kahlil Gibran projects the psychic of those who try to measure their potential externally.

A leader with a Sufi heart can see beyond five senses. 'If you can see only what light reveals and hear only what sound announces, then in truth you do not see nor do you hear,' tells the sage of Lebanon. And Rumi takes you to greater heights, 'Only from the heart can you touch the sky!'.[8]

Leaders must trust the words of Swami Vivekananda, a great Indian Sage: 'All power is within you. You can do anything and everything. Believe in that.' Only leaders with great vision can lead *inside-out*. We call them visionary leaders. They see the world from their inner vision and manage affairs from their inner self.

---

[8] Jelaluddin Rumi, *RUMI Daylight—A Daybook of Spiritual Guidance.*

Open the Love Window.

The moon won't use the door.

Only the window!

—*Rumi*

6

Reach the Heart with 'High-Touch'

You may forget the one with whom you have laughed, but never the one with whom you have wept!
—Kahlil Gibran, *The Greatest Works of Kahlil Gibran*

If doctors have healing touch, there is nothing great. But if a common man has the healing touch, that is great. A leader who does not have a healing touch is not the leader with the Sufi heart. Those who manage *Dil Se* are capable of healing the bleeding hearts and soothing the perturbed souls. Their hearts are filled with tranquillity and they infuse serenity in others.

A leader must learn to get wet his shoulder with the tears of the one whose heart aches. 'How to get wet one's shoulder with the tears of others' was a unique experience I had during a 10-day spiritual convention in San Francisco organised by State of the World Forum on the delicate theme 'Creating a Culture of Peace', where amazingly over 90 per cent participants were from the corporate sector. The delegates came from different parts of the world. On the concluding day the organisers took us to a church, not for grinding the axe for propagating Christianity but to utilise the spacious ground where such a big crowd could find sufficient space. First, they asked to make a big circle by holding hands of each other. I cannot express in words the energy flow, rather the energy current, that was flowing from one body to another. One can find such transmission of soul energy from one body to another in low scale while hugging someone. But while you get linked with hundreds of human beings with physical connectivity, the soul energy just gushes from one body to other.

Later, one of the lady organisers gave a heart-touching sermon, reminding us that we were in togetherness for past 10 days. Once we part would not meet with most of them. Her voice touched the soul, and our hearts were filled with sorrow with the strange feeling of parting that we never thought earlier. Then I heard her whispering sound, 'Can you hug each other without bringing age or sex a barrier'. All of us started hugging each other crying. I don't know how many ladies and men—young and old—wet my shoulder and how many shoulders I wet with a strange feeling of parting with the people who were never important to us till we were made aware of the unique relationship of the 10-day meet.

'Our most sacred tears never seek our eyes,' believes the great Sufi, Kahlil Gibran.[1] They seek the heart of Lord. God loves the sacred tears of His creature. A sacred tear shed in repentance is dearer to God than the lifespan spent in His worship.

Many years have passed. I made a major shift in career from Executive Vice President to Senior Professor in one of the management institutes. While my industrial background was my real strength, the sagacity that I had adopted by infusing spirituality in business management made me different. I cannot forget one incident. One of my junior colleagues, Dr S. Padmaja, who was a learned Assistant Professor, entered my room with swelling eyes filled with tears. It appears she was scolded by the Director on her

[1] Kahlil Gibran, *The Greatest Works of Kahlil Gibran*.

sluggish approach towards the assigned targets. She simply asked, 'Mr Siddiqui, I need your shoulder—I want to cry', and I obliged her with no hesitation. She cried and cried. I didn't ask any question. I could feel the wetness on my shoulder. After sometime I found she was comfortable. Later she shared with me that the Director of the management institute had reprimanded her harshly for not meeting her quarterly targets. We had heart-to-heart talk and she promised that she would never lag in meeting the assigned targets. It was a turning point in her career and an unforgettable moment in my life that revived my faith and confidence in *high-touch*.

Tears are sacred. Tears must be respected. 'There must be something strangely sacred in salt. It is in our tears and in the sea!' A very profound thought of the Sufi of Lebanon, Kahlil Gibran.[2] The largest water body is salty, so are our tears. The teardrop is as sacred as the great ocean. Tears appear to clean the inner self. Tears of penitence open the doors of heavens. Wiping out the tears from the face of mankind is a Godly effort.

> **Tears Are Sacred**
>
> Our God in His gracious thirst will drink us all, the dewdrop and the tear.
> —Kahlil Gibran, *The Greatest Works of Kahlil Gibran*

A leader who does not possess a healing touch is not a leader at all. *High-touch*, or call *healing touch* for a common understanding, is an inescapable prerequisite trait for a leader's success in new age.

Today we are proud of managing High-Tech. While taking pride we forget that you can only manage, you cannot lead 'High Tech', because soulless things cannot be led. In fact, we need leaders with higher level of consciousness to counterbalance the after-effects of high-tech with high-touch.

Over three decades ago, John Naisbitt in his famous book *Megatrends*, published in 1982, first time used the terminology *high-tech* and *high-touch*, envisaging that with advent of 21st century, the

---

[2] Kahlil Gibran, *The Greatest Works of Kahlil Gibran*.

hi-touch would become an essentiality for balancing the surmounting stress, which would be caused by *high-tech*—the advanced technology, which will be spiritually empty. Later, the same author came up with another book entitled *High Tech, High Touch*. In a high-tech world with an increasing search for balance, high-touch will be the key to differentiate products and services as well as the quality of leadership. Focusing on the effects of technology in re-shaping society, the book brought together a mountain of evidence implicating technology in relentlessly accelerating human lives and stirring profound yearnings for a more emotionally satisfying existence. The new age organisations, espousing sophisticated technology, shall be a great challenge to the leadership—technology will create more stress. This *high-tech stress* can be counterbalanced only with *high-touch*. As the technology grows, *high-touch* in leadership will become an inescapable necessity.

The new age is the product of our *mind-power*. Mind is restless you cannot control it. Swami Rama, an Indian sage, explains the tendency of mind beautifully:

> *Many people think the mind can be controlled. That is not a useful idea. Like the monkey, the mind can never actually be controlled; it can only be directed. If you want to try to control your mind, you will regret the results. Forget the word 'control' and learn to direct your mind and energy on all levels.*

Like mind, you do not have any control on this new age. In fact the new age is controlling the mankind. Today, technology has become the goddess of worship.

Do not trust technology. Do not rely too much on technology—it is spiritually empty. Technology has brought us closer to death. It is the human mind that has created technology. As you know, technology has no heart. Technology has no soul. The users must become aware of this fact and use their innate wisdom to fill the void. Use it with full awareness to the extent it benefits you and mankind, not beyond.

We think through our mind, not through our heart. We trust our mind, not our heart. It is time to trust the heart. It is time to think through the heart. It is time to act through the heart.

Happiness of your people should be the purpose of management. Your *fixed assets* are not your real assets. Your people are your real assets. People are not machines. People are not cattle. All men and women—whom we call employees in business termi-

> **Lead Dil Se...**
>
> It is with the heart one sees rightly; what is essential is visible to the eye.
>
> —Antoine de Saint-Exupery

nology—are the children of humanity. The *silent majority* has the real power. Your people have power to make your business house beautiful. Let us strive to create happiness. Let us reincarnate a new corporate world—*a decent corporate world.*

Kahlil Gibran, a great Sufi of Lebanon, was aware of the challenges of new world that would emerge after his death. '*Healing Touch* will get you the Nirvana,' was his neat belief. 'Yes, there is a Nirvana; it is in leading your sheep to a green pasture, and in putting your child to sleep [with high touch]'.[3]

High-touch should not remain within the confines of thoughts or expression of thoughts; high-touch should be seen and felt in one's actions. Good and noble thoughts are not enough: 'Every thought I have imprisoned in expression I must free by my deeds'.[4]

Today, both in political and corporate lives the leaders, CEOs as well as managers are suffering from depression owing to unmanageable stress. Many a time my consulting company, Intellects Biz, has been asked to conduct workshops on Stress Management. They look for curing the effect without understanding its cause. On the other hand, if a person receives the Divine Bliss and he gradually withdraws himself from the worldly mad race, he is considered as mentally retarded. Such wise person with divine wisdom

---

[3] Kahlil Gibran, *The Greatest Works of Kahlil Gibran.*
[4] Ibid.

is considered as mad. Al-Ghazali, the Sufi of 12th century, nicely explains this bitter truth through his Sufi thoughts:

> *If a man ceases to take any concern in worldly matters, conceives a distaste for common pleasures, and appears sunk in depression, the doctor will say, "This is a case of melancholy, and requires such and such prescription." The physicist will say, "This is a dryness of the brain caused by hot weather and cannot be relieved till the air becomes moist." The Astrologer will attribute it to some particular conjunction or opposition of planets…. It doesn't occur to them that what has really happened is this: that the Almighty has a concern for the welfare of that man, and has therefore commanded His servants, the planets or the elements, to produce such a condition in him that he may turn away from the World to his Maker. The knowledge of this fact is a lustrous pearl from the ocean of inspirational knowledge, to which all other forms of knowledge are as islands in the sea.*[5]

The changing global business scenario is creating a great impact on the minds of authors. Ken Blanchard who started his career with *One Minute Manager* is now writing books of *high-touch* like *The Heart of Leadership, Whale Don, Gung-ho*. The books like *The Monk who Sold his Ferrari* are touching the sale figure in millions. Why? Because today's leaders and managers need such books which can soothe the heart and heal the soul.

Today we have become the part of a mad rush—everyone is running without knowing the destination. Many are involved in some sort of rat race. If at all you want to become the part of race, better compete for acquiring knowledge, wisdom and virtue superior than others. Do not be jealous of someone's material success, envy the knowledge, wisdom and virtue of people and try to acquire higher than others. Al-Ghazali explains this never-ending truth: 'The life of the heart is knowledge; so preserve it. The death of heart is ignorance, so avoid it. Your best provision is true devotion, so provide it. The advice of mine is enough for you, so heed it.'

Do not chase the mirage; mirage is not truth. Race and compete in discovering the truth—the truth that makes the life worth

---

[5] Al-Ghazali, *The Alchemy of Happiness.*

living and worth leading! Race with others by letting others' wounds bleeding in your heart.

Sometimes you get into a blue mood for no reason. It happens to me, it happens to you and everyone who has a soul. Our soul is God's breath, and there has got to be some connectivity.

Sometimes during your happy moments you felt like crying. You struggle to prevent the tears, which are ready to roll down from swollen eyes. There is no cause yet your eyes get wet. You do not know why!

This happens because we are not only human beings but also *inter-beings* or *connected beings*. Our sorrows and joys are not only ours! Others' sorrows and joys also live in our heart. Sometimes our heart beats for others and sometimes in another's heart you find your life flows. Sometimes your heart bleeds from your sorrows and sometimes others' wounds bleed in your heart. Saadi Sherazi, a great Sufi, explains this tendency in one of his Sufi poems—'Gulsitan':

Human beings are members of a whole,
In creation of one essence and soul!
If one member is afflicted with pain,
Other members uneasy will remain.
If you have no empathy for human pain,
The name of human you cannot retain.[6]

How can we fight and cut the parts of our own body? Like human body with many limbs is the mankind as one progeny of a single father with many heads and limbs. Love each of them as you love each part of your body.

'We are not human beings having a spiritual experience,' insists Ken Blanchard, 'We are spiritual beings having a human experience.' We are soul, not a body. Our soul knows this truth but not the body or the mind. Where does the soul dwell? It dwells in the heart and its luxurious dwelling is, a *Sufi heart* where it can get nurtured, nourished and enriched.

[6] Saadi Sherazi, *Gulsitan*.

Power of High Touch

'When somebody is unkind to you, unroll the panorama of his good qualities and hug him or her in your imagination.

Sit down quietly, meditate and pray for his well being. Recall, how many times that person has given you support.

These positive energies will transform into positive responses.'

—K.S. Raju, Chairman, Nagarjuna Group

I have worked in many organisations in the public sector, private sector and also in one of the management institutes. I have worked with many bosses who were very competent and some of them were good leaders. Each of them had some positive qualities, but when it comes to *high-touch*, I found it in only one boss—K.S. Raju, Chairman of Nagarjuna Group. He is a very serene personality, who would never get perturbed. He is a very positive person and his very presence fills the space with positive energies. He has something in him that I cannot explain. When my daughter was getting married, he visited the function hall and desired that he wanted to meet the bride. I escorted him to the ladies section where my daughter was sitting as a bride. He extended his good wishes and prayed using the words that touched everyone's heart. Then he touched her head offering blessings. I wish I could have remembered those words.

Have you ever noticed that when you help a lame duck and apply some balm on its wounds, you feel as if your own wounds are being healed! When you curse someone, you turn accursed. When you insult someone, you stand in contempt. How strange!

If you are angry and kick someone, you kick none but yourself. Kick the fellow again and again, as many times as you deserve to be kicked. 'How strange that yet we spit on our own faces,' says Kahlil Gibran, 'not once but many times!'.[7]

Leading with *high-touch* is possible only when you develop a *Sufi heart* in your leadership by moving from lower levels to the higher levels of consciousness. Expand your leadership consciousness and prevent it from contraction.

[7] Kahlil Gibran, *The Greatest Works of Kahlil Gibran.*

The world, indeed, is like a dream and the treasures of the world are an alluring mirage! Like the apparent distances in a picture, things have no reality in themselves, but they are like heat haze.

—Buddha

7

STOP CHASING THE MIRAGE

We measure time according to the movement of countless suns; and they measure
time by little machine in their little pockets. Now tell me how could we ever meet
at the same place and the same time?
—KAHLIL GIBRAN, *THE GREATEST WORKS OF KAHLIL GIBRAN*

Once, I was returning after conducting a session in Centre for Organization Development (COD) on softer aspects of business management, one of the participants wanted a lift. I obliged. Later I realised that the real purpose was not just getting a drop; the real purpose was seeking certain clarification and guidance in the matter of value-based management.

'Sir, why did you say that the value of a currency note depends on the mode of its earning?'

I explained my logic:

The value of money is not What you have earned; *the value of money largely depends on,* How you have earned. *The ill-gotten money harms beyond lifetime. The impact of ill-gotten money lasts long and it spoils many generations. Sometimes God punishes us by withdrawing wealth and sometimes*

by pouring it beyond our needs. Wealth is good when it comes in moderation.
The same wealth becomes curse when it becomes in excess. The ill-gotten
money corrupts you and your next generations.

He was very much impressed. After a bit hesitation he chose
to share with me some of his personal secrets. He mentioned that
before getting into the service in bank, he wanted to become a
bureaucrat. He attempted IAS but could not succeed. His ambition was not to make a career in government service—his ambition was to amass wealth through corrupt means. 'Power corrupts;
absolute power corrupts absolutely,' he shared. 'I wanted the absolute powers to make a good fortune. I was very frustrated as I
could not fulfil my dream—my mission to amass ill-gotten wealth
failed.'

I didn't stop him. His story was interesting. He was honestly
sharing his bleeding heart.

> **No Meeting Point**
>
> Your mind and my heart will
> never agree until your mind
> ceases to live in number and
> my heart in the mist.
>
> —Kahlil Gibran,
> *The Greatest Works of*
> *Kahlil Gibran*

Sir, today I got wisdom from your session. I felt very relieved. I am fully convinced that values play an important role not only in business but also in our personal lives. I promise, I will never hold such dreams. Though I have opportunity to make a few more attempts, but I shall not avail them. I am happy with this job—I am getting a moderate salary, but my life is peaceful.

Greed and *tranquillity* are stepsisters. They cannot dwell together.
Greed settles in the mind and tranquillity in the heart. Greed looks
for numbers; tranquillity for fantasies. There is no meeting point
for dwellers of heart and dwellers of mind.

Today many people wish to become leaders to loot the country
and countrymen. Professional managers wish to climb the ladder
of hierarchy to gain more and more power for making material

gains. Leaders, both in politics and corporate sector, want to secure absolute power to become corrupt absolutely. The leaders are corrupt because the systems that we have formulated are corrupt. If a person is required to spend in millions to get the position of power in a democratic country, he has to reap it after making such heavy investments. Likewise, when a young guy has to pay heavy donations to get a seat in medicines or engineering, his first aim is to get it back by hook or by crook. One tries to gain power to get corrupt. The taste of power is the taste of blood. Once one gets addicted, he or she turns into a vampire.

India is no exception; rather, it is one of the leading countries in corruption. Earlier we used to hear of political scams in terms of millions or billions. Today the volume of scams has become so huge that even your pocket calculator is incapable to show the number on the screen. One corrupt party points out finger to the other. But, after sometime, when the accusing party is exposed by the accused, it withdraws the charges coolly. Even the responsible ministers make most irresponsible remarks: *People's memory is very short, they cannot remember such scams for long.*

> **Look at Your Faults First...**
>
> Anyone who sees their own faults before noticing those of others, why don't they correct themselves? People of the world don't look at themselves, and so they blame one another.
>
> —Jelaluddin Rumi, *RUMI Daylight—A Daybook of Spiritual Guidance*

Many activists and saintly Babas attract masses and take a public vow to eradicate corruption and raise slogans to get back the black treasure hidden in the Swiss Banks. But when their balloons are punctured, they fall from the heights like wingless birds. When everyone is corrupt, who will blaspheme whom? Almost all political leaders with a negligible exception lead with the physical or egoistic perspectives. I am not talking only about Indian politics; I am talking about global politics.

Today our minds and souls are corrupted with materialism in capitalistic societies. We have lost the purpose of life. We have lost the wisdom to make a distinction between the container and the content.

In olden China in a great monastery, the Zen master organized the dinner for new students on the very first day. The first item was soup. He provided many types of soup-bowls made of porcelain, clay, glass, crystal, some plain looking, some expansive, some exquisite—asking the disciples to help themselves.

When all the students had a bowl of soup in hand, the Zen Master said: "If you noticed, all the nice looking expensive soup bowls were taken up, leaving behind the plain and cheap ones. While it is normal for you to want only the best for yourselves, that reflects our lust for greed—I should have better than others. Be assured that the bowl itself adds no value to the soup. What all of you really wanted was soup, not the cup, but you consciously went for the best bowl…. And then you began eyeing each other's bowls. Now consider this: Life is the soup; money and social status are the bowls. *The good-looking expensive bowls cannot add any flavor to the quality of soup. They are just tools to hold and contain life and the type of bowl we have does not define, nor change the quality of life we live. Sometimes, by concentrating only on the bowl, we fail to enjoy the soup that God had provided to us."*

Like the soup-bowl, the water tumbler is a container. It is not the tumbler but water that quenches our thirst. Even the tumbler of gold cannot quench the thirst—it can only satisfy your greed. But greed cannot serve the purpose of life. Most mistakenly most of us think the purpose of life is to get something from it. What we do not understand is that what life gives to us in the material form is just transitory. We *know* this yet do not *realise*—we tend to become wilfully blind to this naked fact.

Today, everyone is running without knowing why he or she is running. If you ask someone, 'Why are you running?' you will get the answer, 'I really do not know. I am running because everyone else is running!' We acquired speed but lost our sense of direction. We are speeding along without any clues. Speeding along with heedlessness leads one to disaster—which we are already in. We have already lost the way.

Why? This is because most of us have morphed into *clock managers*! We keep looking at the watch and try to manage our activities within the available time slot. We are taught to 'Do things Right!' We are not taught to 'Do Right things!' Today, the corporate world is suffering because we do not groom anyone into being a *compass manager*—one who will show us the direction. Today's corporate world is suffering because we do not have *Sufi managers* who will tell us what is right and what is wrong. The modern day corporate world is suffering because we are guided by *management gurus* who keep an eye on the bottom line while the *management monks*, who can show us the righteous path, are unbelievably in short supply. It is high time to look for management monks.

Following is an anecdote, which conveys an important moral about the quality of life.

A boat docked in a tiny Mexican fishing village. A tourist, who was a management Guru, complimented the local fishermen on the quality of their fish and asked how long it took them to catch the fish.

'Not very long,' they answered in unison.

'Why didn't you stay out longer and catch more?' asked the Guru. The fishermen explained that their small catches were sufficient to meet their needs and those of their families.

'But what do you do with the rest of your time?' asked the management Guru.

'We sleep late, fish a little, play with our children, and take a siesta with our wives. In the evening, we go into the village to see our friends, have a few drinks, play the guitar, and sing a few songs. We live a wholesome happy life.'

'I am a management Guru from Harvard Business School and I can help you!' the Guru interrupted. 'You should start by fishing longer every day. You can then sell the extra fish you catch. With the extra revenue, you can buy a bigger boat.' He paused and continued with his unsolicited advice, 'And after that, with the extra money the larger boat will bring, you can buy a second one

and a third one and so on until you have an entire fleet of trawlers. Instead of selling your fish to a middleman, you can then negotiate directly with the fish processing plants. Soon you may even open your own plant. You can then leave this little village and move to Mexico City, Los Angeles, or even New York City! From there you can direct your huge new enterprise.' After his sermon, he looked at the fishermen expecting some good words from them. Instead, one fisherman asked.

'How long would that take?'

'Twenty, perhaps twenty-five years,' replied the Guru.

'And after that?' asked the same man.

'After that? Well my friend, that's when it gets really interesting,' answered the Guru, thoughtlessly. Obviously he was not ready for such a question from these ignorant fishermen. However, he promptly replied, 'When your business gets really big, you can start buying and selling stocks and make millions!'

'Millions! Really? And after that?' asked the same fisherman.

'After that, you'll be able to retire, live in a tiny village near the coast, sleep late, play with your children, catch a few fish, take a siesta with your wife and spend your evenings drinking and enjoying with your friends.'

'With all due respect, Sir,' retorted the Mexican fisherman, 'but that's exactly what we are doing now. So what's the point of wasting twenty-five years?' The management Guru was clueless and did not know what to reply!

Today we are in mad rat race. One must understand that the winner in a rat race remains a rat! Know where you are going in life. Who knows you may already be there! When you run directionless, you cannot reach the destination. Heedlessness along with greed is causing incalculable damage to society as well as to the corporate world. Greed has barricaded the world with hatred. These barricades must break. The loving hearts must replace the cunning minds. We think too much and feel too little. Leadership needs a mega-shift from physical and egoistic perspectives to love and Sufi perspective.

How to heal the heart with full of greed? Let me quote an anecdote, how Mulla Nasurdin teaches a lesson to a person who was very greedy.

Mulla Nasrudin borrowed a pot from his friend, who was a very greedy person. The next day, he gave the friend back the pot, plus another smaller pot.

The friend looked at the small pot, and said, 'What's that?'

'Your pot gave birth while I had it,' said Nasrudin, 'so I am giving you its child.'

The friend, happy to receive the bonus, did not ask another question.

A week later, Nasrudin once again borrowed the original pot from the friend.

After a week passed, the friend asked Nasrudin to return it.

'I can't,' said Nasrudin.

'Why not?' the friend asked.

'Well,' Nasrudin answered, 'I hate to be the bearer of bad news ... but your pot has died.'

'What?' the friend asked with skepticism. 'A pot can't die!'

'Well, you believed it gave birth,' said Nasrudin, 'so is why is it that you can't believe it died?'

Choosing money for mental peace is not a good bargain. 'Emotional attachment to maya is totally painful; this is a bad bargain,' says a great Indian Sufi, Guru Nanak. India and Indians would not have suffered with scam-based politics had we followed Guru Nanak's wisdom and his approach towards the worldly affairs.

Virtue

that which brings peace to your mind and tranquillity to your soul.

Vice

that which makes your heart flutter and which throws your soul in perturbation.
—Prophet Mohammed, *Imam Bukhari's Hadeez*

The foundation of today's capitalistic society is greed—everyone is running over the bodies chasing the mirage. 'What they say competitive edge,' to my mind, it is gaining the edge over others' greed! There is a mad rush. Money, money, money—means have lost their meaning. Earlier the political scams were worth thousands, today worth millions and billions! A leader whose purpose of existence is *material gains* is not a leader at all. The one who cannot understand the true purpose of life is not worth living, let alone worth leading. It sounds a bit loud, but I mean it. Leaders with their eyes on the material gains will end up in terrible pains. Those who cannot lead their own lives cannot lead others'.

Greed leads to *jealousy*. Only greedy people are jealous of others. Jealousy generates hatred, which engulfs the families and societies. Both, greed and jealousy stop progress in society. 'If you could unite your wings and free your soul of jealousy, you and everyone around you would fly up like doves,' says Rumi.[1]

Contentedness is the seat of happiness. When you look up, the sky is too high to reach but when you look down, you can see the ground realities. *Contentedness* is known as *Tawakkul* in Arabic, which grants happiness. Let me quote another anecdote of Mulla Nasrudin, a Sufi, known for his inimitability.

Mulla Nasrudin was talking to his neighbor one day, and the neighbor lamented, "I'm really having trouble fitting my family in our small house. It's me, my wife, my three kids, and my mother-in-law—all sharing the same cottage. Mulla Nasrudin, you are a wise man. Do you have any advice for me?"

"Yes," replied Nasrudin. "Do you have any chickens in your yard?"

"I have ten," the man replied.

"Put them in the house," said Nasrudin.

"But Mulla," the man remarked, "our house is already cramped as it is."

"Just try it," replied Nasrudin.

[1] Jelaluddin Rumi, *RUMI Daylight—A Daybook of Spiritual Guidance.*

The man, desperate to find a solution to his spacing woes, followed Nasrudin's advice, and paid him another visit the next day.

"Mulla," he said, "things are even worse now. With the chickens in the house, we are even more pressed for space."

"Now take that donkey of yours," replied Nasrudin, "and bring it in the house." The man bemoaned and objected, but Nasrudin convinced him to do it.

The next day, the man, now looking more distressed than ever, came up to Nasrudin and said, "Now my home is even more crowded! Between my family, the chickens, and that donkey of mine, there is barely any room to move."

"Well then," said Nasrudin, "do you have any other animals in your yard?"

"Yes," the man replied, "we have a goat."

"OK," said the other. "Take the goat in your house too."

The man once again raised a fuss and seemed anything but eager to follow Nasrudin's advice, but Nasrudin once again convinced him to put yet another animal in the house.

The next day, the man, now full of anger and annoyance came up to Nasrudin and exclaimed, "My family is really upset now. Everyone is at my throat complaining about the lack of space. Your plan is making us miserable."

"OK," Nasrudin replied, "now take all of the animals back outside."

So the man followed his advice, and the next day, he dropped by Nasrudin and remarked, "Mulla-your plan has worked like a charm. With all the animals out, my house is so spacious that none of us can help but being pleased and uncomplaining."

Most of us lack *contentedness* and become unhappy by keeping the focus on *what is not there*, without realising or appreciating the worth of what is there. Most of us mistake the purpose of life as gaining pleasure by avoiding pains. No, the purpose of life is not gaining pleasure and avoiding pains. The purpose of life is to find meaning in pleasure and pains. Be grateful to God, both in pleasure and pains—when have pleasure thank Him; when pass through a crucial phase of life, be steadfast and hold patience.

'Pain is a treasure, for it contains God's Mercies,' says Rumi, the sage. How true. Sometime we mistake the blessings as pains. 'When someone beats a rug, the blows are not against the rug, but against the dust in it,' explains Rumi. One should not run away from the hour of tests, rather take them boldly. 'The moon stays bright when it doesn't avoid the night,' says Rumi. He further guides us: 'When you go through a hard period, when everything seems to oppose you, when you feel you cannot even bear one more minute, never give up. Because, it is the time and place that the course will divert!'.[2] And when your patience grants you the dividend, remember God and extend your gratitude to Him.

Man by his nature is selfish. We remember God when in pain and forget Him in pleasure. Kabir Das, an Indian Sufi, grants us wisdom in these words: 'While suffering everyone prays and remembers Him, in joy no one does; If one prays and remembers Him in happiness, why would sorrow come?'

Sometime we *manufacture* sorrows in modern factories. We produce the products that are harmful to mankind. Yet we take pleasure and pride in such products of destruction. The world is beautiful. Do not spoil it by developing products and services that are not good for mankind. We have lost the way. Greed has overpowered us. We have given this world hatred, bloodshed and miseries. We have made our knowledge cynical. Our thinking has gone skewed. We work like machines and robots. We have no time to think. We have no time to act. We do little for our people and mankind.

Today we need humility more than cleverness. We need kindness and gentleness. We need to shower love and mercy upon people. Don't look what you don't have; look what you have and be happy.

The only remedy to heal the world and corporate world is to discover the leaders and corporate managers who have the Sufi

[2] Jelaluddin Rumi, *RUMI Daylight—A Daybook of Spiritual Guidance*.

hearts—the heart free from the worldly greed and filled with love for mankind.

The Sufi thoughts of Al-Ghazali, a great Sufi of 13th century, direct us, proscribing and prescribing the guiding principles, which will lead us to success:

> *Each of your breaths is a priceless jewel, since each of them is irreplaceable and, once gone, can never be retrieved. Do not be like the deceived fools who are joyous because each day their wealth increases while their life shortens. What good is an increase in wealth when life grows ever shorter? Therefore be joyous only for an increase in Knowledge or in good works, for they are your two best companions who will accompany you in your grave when your family, wealth, children and friends stay behind.*[3]

Through these pages I remind these misleaders about the great warrior who got wisdom before the angel of death visited him. He was Alexander the Great. He was the disciple of the great philosopher, Aristotle.

As per one tradition, the famous warrior, Alexander the Great, left a noble message for mankind. One can learn many lessons from the following legend:

> *The great Greek warrior, Alexander, after conquering many kingdoms, was returning home. On the way, he fell ill and he was bedridden for months. With death drawing close, Alexander realized how his conquests, his great army, his sharp sword and all his wealth—the precious gifts that he had received from Life—were of no use.*
>
> *He called his Generals and said, "My time has come and I will depart from this world soon. But I have three wishes. Please fulfil my wishes without fail." With tears flowing down their cheeks, the Generals agreed to abide by their King's last wishes.*
>
> *"My first desire is that," said Alexander, "my physicians alone must carry my coffin." "Secondly, when my coffin is being carried to the grave, the path leading to the graveyard should be strewn with gold, silver and precious stones which I have collected in my treasury. My third and last wish is that both my*

[3] Al-Ghazali, *The Alchemy of Happiness*.

hands should be kept dangling out of my coffin." The people who had gathered there were amazed at the King's strange wishes. Yet no one dared to question the King. Alexander's favourite General kissed his hand and pressed them to his heart. "O King, we assure you that your wishes will all be fulfilled. But tell us why do you make such strange wishes?"

At this Alexander took a deep breath and said, "I would like the world to know of the three lessons I have learnt at the fag-end of my Life—just at this moment. I want my physicians to carry my coffin because people should realize that no doctor can ever give Life to anybody. They are powerless and cannot save a person from the clutches of death. So let not people take life for granted.

The second wish of strewing gold, silver and other riches on the way to the graveyard is to tell people that not even a fraction of gold can be taken with me. Let people realize that it is a sheer waste of time to chase worldly wealth.

And about my third wish, of having my hands dangling out of the coffin, I want people to know that I came empty handed into this world and empty handed I go out of this world."

Etch in stone Alexander's last words: "Bury my body, do not build any monument; while taking my coffin keep my hands outside so that the world knows the person who won the world had nothing in his hands when dying".

What you take from life remains with the world; what you give to life remains with you forever in the life after this worldly life. This reminds me of the famous Rabbi—Rabbi Hafez Ayim. Once an American tourist went to Cairo to visit Rabbi Hafez. The American tourist was surprised to see that the Rabbi lived in a simple room, filled with books, in which the only pieces of furniture were a table and a stool. 'Rabbi, where is your furniture?' the tourist asked. 'And where is yours?' Hafez retorted. 'Mine? I don't need, I am just passing through,' replied the tourist. 'So am I,' said the Rabbi.

Remembrance of death makes people sober. Once we understand the temporal nature of world and temporary status of life, we become sober and humble towards mankind. Their heads will not swell with pride and ego, which make a leader, a *misleader*.

There is no place for pride and ego in the Sufi heart. There is not a single Sufi who has not condemned these tendencies by reminding man his death—the eventual reality. They often remind mankind to remember their temporary status in the world. 'I am a bird of the heavenly garden, I belong not to the earthly sphere,' writes Rumi with poetic fervour. 'They have made for two or three days a cage of my body.'

Kabir Das, an India Sufi, compares death with the beautiful bird swan, which will fly to sky sooner or later. Kabir Das has always reminded mankind to understand the life realities. Let me quote a few Kabi's *dohe*:

'Kabir, Don't be so proud and vain, looking at your high mansion;
Tomorrow you will lie under feet, on top will grow grass!'

'When you came in to this world, everyone laughed while you cried;
Don't do such deeds that they may laugh when you are gone!'

'If you are Big, so what? Just like a date tree!
No shade for travellers? Fruits are hard to reach.'

'Alive one sees, alive one knows, find your liberation while alive;
If 'alive' you do not cut the noose of your attachment, how will there be
liberation from death?'

'Speak such words, you lose the mind's Ego;
Body remains composed, others find Peace!'

When you speak, kill your ego so it is not reflected in your speech. Don't brag, don't gloat, don't make yourself out to be big, rich or important or anything else that reflects your ego. If ego is avoided in one's speech, the listener finds peace from listening to it.

Today we live in the mad, mad, mad world. The corporate world is no sane world. In this world the profane appears to be sacred and the corrupt looks honest. Instead of hiding their shame they wish others should shrug away their shame and become shameless. The gays want the world should follow the gay practices and the lesbians are busy preaching their outlook as the symbol of true freedom. The gamblers want people to become gamblers and the drunkards' wishes are no different. The addicts want the entire world must get addicted and the worshippers of Satan want to convert the pious people.

The leaders want their sons to grow with greed, and, if not all, many actors and actresses wish their children to grow under their shameless shadow of fame. Pornography is a well-accepted industry—the porn artists wish their daughters to gain edge over others' bareness. Even the princesses are in race to pose *topless* and *bottomless*! Why should we, then, curse a prostitute who trains her young daughter to grow up to be a sexy call girl—an upgraded version of the age-old profession?

Today people with Sufi Sagacity are in minority—they are *odd-man-out*! And those who talk about Sufi Sagacity in leadership are no different!

Kahlil Gibran compares this world with a madhouse where everyone is trying others to look like him. Most strangely and amazingly, the mad people consider sages and Sufis as the dwellers of madhouse.

It was in the garden of a madhouse that I met a youth with a face pale and lovely and full of wonder.

And I sat beside him upon the bench, and I said, 'Why are you here?'

And he looked at me in astonishment, and he said, 'It is an unseemly question, yet I will answer you. My father would make of me a reproduction of himself; so also my uncle. My mother would have me the image of her illustrious father. My sister would hold up her seafaring husband as the perfect example for me to follow. My brother thinks I should be like him, a fine athlete. And my teachers also, the doctor of philosophy, and the music-master, and the logician, they too were determined, and each would have me but a reflection of his own face in the mirror. Therefore I came to his place. I find it more sane here. At least, I can be myself.' Then of a sudden he turned to me and said, 'But tell me, were you also driven to this place by education and good counsel?'

And I answered, 'No, I am a visitor.'

And he said, 'Oh, you are one of those who live in the madhouse on the other side of the wall?'

If we examine our life carefully, many of us have got corrupted, yet we feel we are honest. Why we feel so? Because we live among the people who are no different! In madhouse, no one considers himself mad. Rather, the people who live other side of fence appear mad.

What appears to be truthful may not be truthful. What appears to be mirage may not be mirage? Many suffer from optic illusion—many suffer from mental delusion. And many are chasing mirage assuming they are visionary. Many are misleading unknowingly; many are misleading knowingly. The latter are real danger to society and corporate world.

Stop *chasing the mirage*. No one has ever conquered it!

It is not how much we give but how much love we put into giving.

—Mother Teresa

8

GENEROSITY IN LEADERSHIP

You owe more than gold to him who serves you. Give him your heart or serve him.
—KAHLIL GIBRAN, *THE GREATEST WORKS OF KAHLIL GIBRAN*

After retiring from active politics Winston Churchill never looked back to politics. He engaged himself in gardening and acquiring knowledge of Bible. Once one of his old friends visited him. He was shocked to see that the former Prime Minister of Great Britain was polishing his shoes.

"You polish your shoes?" He asked.

"Yes, I polish my shoes, not others'," was the witty response of Churchill. Then he asked his friend, "Don't you polish your shoes?"

"No, I don't polish my shoes. My servant polishes my shoes," proudly replied his friend.

"It is worse than polishing others' shoes," replied Winston Churchill.

Great leaders are not only humble but also have great value for human dignity.

Leadership is service not status. Great leaders are servants not bosses. They are giver and not takers. Generosity is one of the traits of good leadership. They have great concern for their people. They are kind and generous.

I am tempted to quote a famous Sanskrit proverb which reads as follows: 'He who allows his day by without practicing generosity and enjoying life's pleasures is like blacksmith's bellows—he breathes but does not live.' Living selfishly is akin to death; living selflessly is akin to life.

The Giver Is Taker

If you help others with sincere motivation and sincere concern, that will bring you more fortune, more friends, more smiles, and more success. If you forget about others' rights and neglect others' welfare, ultimately you will be lonely.

—Dalai Lama, *An Open Heart—Practicing Compassion in Everyday Life*

A leader is a giver, not a taker. To my mind this is the *touch stone*. When I scan Indian leaders, I find only one soul, who was the giver. It was Mohandas Karamchand Gandhi. He was a giver, not a taker. He gave his life and got us freedom, but never looked for any position of power or status. Today's politicians talk about Gandhism superficially, without understanding the attributes of his leadership.

Sant Tukaram—a saint and Marathi poet—writes: 'Can water drink itself? Can a tree taste its own fruit?' The answer is 'No'. Then, how can a leader lead for gaining self-benefit? If this simple wisdom touches the heart of the leaders the entire world will change.

Alas! We find no such wisdom in today's leaders either in politics or in business sector. Everyone wants the positions of high status for self-enjoyment not for serving others. A heart that doesn't beat for others is not a heart at all. Give it some other name.

Believe it or not, giving is gaining! It benefits both, the taker as well as the giver. The recipient is benefited from the gift of the giver and the giver gets the benefit by virtue of having been a *giver*.

Sometimes the giver can see the gains immediately after giving and sometimes the benefits will occur after many years. Whatever you give, your time, money, charity, physical help, supportive words, will create a positive impact on the giver. This positive impact of giving remains long even after one's death.

The giver gains; the giver never loses. 'Not only the thirsty seeks the water,' believes Rumi, 'the water as well seeks the thirsty!'.[1] These softer aspects of life we understand not. Giving is not losing; giving is gaining.

Giving is a great virtue. *Giver* is a leader; *taker* is not. If at all a leader wants to take from his people, let him take their sorrows, tears and wounds to heal. Let him borrow their problems to solve. Let him take their good wishes and greetings for his own success!

'You give but little when give of your possessions. It is when you give of yourself that you truly give,' believes Kahlil Gibran.[2] Many of us do not give for protecting their tomorrow. 'For what are your possessions but things you keep and guard for fear you may need them tomorrow? And tomorrow, what shall tomorrow bring to the over-prudent dog burying bones in the trackless sand as he follows the pilgrims to the holy city?' Tomorrow is uncertain. If dog buries the bones in the trackless sands, he would never find it; likewise, the wealth saved without giving the poor persons' share from such hording will disappear for no cause.

A giver gains in many ways:

- It can make a positive difference to others—even when you through one star fish out of million which lie on beach to die, it makes the difference to the one which is thrown into the ocean safely.
- It can help you achieve your fullest potential—when you make efforts to help others, you have got to stretch your potential to acquire more resources.

[1] Jelaluddin Rumi, *RUMI Daylight—A Daybook of Spiritual Guidance.*
[2] Kahlil Gibran, *The Greatest Works of Kahlil Gibran.*

- It can help in providing a purpose or meaning to your life—the life without a purpose or a meaning is not worth living.
- It provides the inner joy and happiness—it heals the wounds of others soothes the soul of the giver.
- Recent scientific studies have proved that a *giver* can never get into the mental depression. Rather, the power of giving can cure those who suffer from mental depression.

It is better to give a needy who comes to you. But there are many people who are needy but too shy to spread their hands. 'It is well to give when asked, but it is better to give unasked, through understanding,' is the neat advice of the Sufi of Lebanon.[3]

There are those who give little of the much which they have—and they give it for recognition and their hidden desire makes their gifts unwholesome. And there are those who have little and give it all. These are the believers in life and the bounty of life, and their coffer is never empty.

It is difficult to understand this sagacity for a common man, but those who give for helping the deserved never become poor. I may quote a parable, which is quite relevant.

In olden days there was rich man who was known for helping others. A good portion of his earning he used to spend for supporting others. He constructed a huge building at the roadside where the travellers can take shelter during their journey; take food, rest and then move. While leaving the shelter place the travellers were given the packed snacks and a water bottle so that on their way they should not remain hungry or thirsty. Gradually his inn became popular.

One of his advisers advised him that if he continues his charity like this his entire wealth will finish and he would turn pauper. The rich man was quite impressed by his advice. But his wife was not quite impressed. She declined to agree with her husband's advisor. But her husband took the advice

[3] Kahlil Gibran, *The Greatest Works of Kahlil Gibran.*

seriously—A wealthy man is ruined through his misdirected charity. *He started gradually controlling his expenses on charity. When people were not respected and given the inhospitable treatment they stopped halting there. Gradually the Inn lost its popularity. His wife was watching all that was happening helplessly with a bleeding heart.*

Once the couple had gone to their farm at the outskirts. It was a pleasant day. His wife came near the well and leaned over the parapet wall to see its depth. Then she requested her husband to call the farmer and ask him to pull water for irrigating the plants. His husband asked the farmer to do so. Every time the farmer pulled out the water using his two buffaloes, she would lean over the wall and look at the water inside the well. This continued for sometime. Her husband was looking at her crazy wife watchfully. But she never looked at him and continued looking at the water every time the farmer pulled out gallons of water for irrigation. After some time her husband enquired, what she was trying to see looking deep into the well? She didn't respond for sometime and remained still looking at the depth of water. After sometime, she asked her husband to follow her. He also leaned over the wall and looked at the water but didn't understand why his wife asked him to do so! His wife asked him, "Are you seeing the water level—has it come down?" Her husband became aware what she was trying to say. He also watched the water for sometime. Though the water level had gone down to begin with, but just after few minutes it came back to its original level. Wisdom struck to him—money spent on others comes back to you as the water is refilled in the well. *He decided never to seek advice from the petty minded people in future. He came back and sacked his advisor and gave order to restore all the charitable means and spend lavishly for helping others.*

Everyone takes water from river but river never fears losing its treasure. River quenches the thirst of human beings and animals. It flows with the same spirit and speed without bothering how much water has been taken away by people for quenching

The *Taker* Helps the *Giver*

It is indeed misery if I stretch an empty hand to men and receive nothing; but it is hopelessness if I stretch a full hand and find none to receive.

—Kahlil Gibran, *The Greatest Works of Kahlil Gibran*

their thirst. Whether you believe it or not, always there is a bright future for those who help others!

Good deeds start with good thoughts. 'Taking the first step with good thought, the second with good words, and the third with good deed, you enter the paradise' explains a famous Persian proverb. By doing good deeds, you become the first beneficiary, the taker is the second beneficiary. In fact, the taker helps the giver by getting him an opportunity to win the heart of the heaven. Imagine the day where there is no taker!

It is believed that among all the human deeds God loves those who serve others' needs. He showers His blessings upon those who serve the mankind.

Have you ever observed when you feel happy within? Is it when you spread your hands and someone gives you something, or is it when someone spreads his hand and you give him with love? Kahlil Gibran, a great Sufi says, 'When giver's hand touches the taker's hand, it touches the heart of God'.[4]

Once Saadi of Shiraz, a great Sufi was sleeping in his small cottage. A thief entered the house, and found nothing there to steal. As he was leaving disappointedly, the dervish perceived his disappointment and threw him the blanket, in which he was sleeping, so that he should not go away empty-handed.

Give with love, never with pride! Give without any expectation—believe me the law of energy response will get you the returns. Giving never goes waste. Learn from nature. 'The Sun never says to the Earth, 'You owe me.' Look what happens with a love like that. It lights up the whole sky,' says a famous Sufi Poet Hafiz.[5]

Train your mind to listen to your Sufi heart not sometimes but always. Heart guards you from the evil. 'There is a piece of flesh in the body that, if it is righteous, ensures that the whole system will be righteous, and if corrupted, the whole body will become corrupt. This piece of flesh is the Heart,' said Prophet Mohammad.[6]

[4] Kahlil Gibran, *The Greatest Works of Kahlil Gibran*.

[5] Hafiz, *Deewan-e-Hafiz*.

[6] Prophet Mohammad, *Imam Bukhari's Hadeez*.

'There are those who give with joy, and that joy is their reward. And there are those who give with pain, and that pain is their baptism,' says Kahlil Gibran.

And there are those who give and know not pain in giving, nor do they seek joy, nor give with mindfulness of virtue. They give as in yonder valley the myrtle breathes its fragrance into space. Trough the hands of such as these God speaks, and from behind their eyes He smiles upon earth.[7]

Many of us are very choosy in giving—we look for giving to the deserved one. The Sufi heart learns from nature. 'You often say, "I would give, but only to the deserving," the trees in your orchard say not so, nor the flocks in your pasture. They give that they may live, for to withhold is to perish'.[8]

The Sufi's advice to leaders is quite simple: 'Generosity is giving more than you can, and pride is taking less than you need.' Alas! We do just opposite to the sage's wisdom. 'Unless life is lived for others, it is not worth living,' says Mother Teresa.

Today we see big posters, hoardings, banners and TV ads making a big show off of small favours done by the leaders or political parties. They give without knowing the art of giving. The real art of giving is that when you give with your right hand your left hand must not know. 'You are indeed charitable when you give,' says the Sufi, 'and while giving turn your face away so that you may not see the shyness of the receiver'.[9]

And another great Sufi, Rumi, teaches the etiquettes to the taker. He says, 'When someone is counting out gold for you, don't look at your hands or the gold. Look at the giver'.[10]

The giver doesn't lose. What he gives, he gets—not immediately, but sooner or later! God gives you more when you give to others. For this reason it is believed that no one can help others

---

[7] Kahlil Gibran, *The Greatest Works of Kahlil Gibran*.

[8] Ibid.

[9] Ibid.

[10] Jelaluddin Rumi, *RUMI Daylight—A Daybook of Spiritual Guidance*.

without helping himself. As mentioned earlier, *not only the thirsty seeks the water, the water as well seeks the thirsty.*

A true story goes as under:

The year was 1863, on a spring day in Northern Pennsylvania. A poor boy was selling good door-to-door to pay his way through school. He realized he had only a dime left, and that he was hungry. So he decided he would ask for a meal at the next house. However, he lost his nerve when a lonely young woman opened the door. Instead of a meal, he asked for a drink of water. She thought he looked hungry and so she brought him a large glass of milk. He drank it slowly, and then, asked, "How much do I owe you?"

You don't owe me anything, she replied. "Mother has taught us never to accept pay for a kindness." He said, "Then I thank you from my heart." As Howard Kelly left that house, he not only strongly physically, but his faith in God and man was strengthened also. He had been ready to give up and quit.

Years later, that young woman became critically ill. The local doctors were baffled. They finally sent her to the big city, where they called in specialist to study her rare disease. Dr Howard Kelly was called in for the consultation. When he heard the name of the town she came from, he went down the hall of the hospital to her room. Dressed in his doctor's gown, he went in to see her. He recognized her at once. He went back to the consultation room determined to do his best to save her life. From that day, he gave special attention.

After a long struggle, the battle was won. Dr Kelly requested from the business office to pass the final billing to him for approval. He looked at it, then wrote something on the edge, and the bill was sent to her room. She feared to open it, for she was sure it would take the rest of her life to pay for it all. Finally, she looked, and something caught her attention on the side of the bill. She read those words:

"Paid in full with one glass of Milk…"

(signed)
Dr Howard Kelly

Generosity pays, not sometimes, always! Generosity is time tested and is practised from time immemorial. There are hundreds of stories which can be quoted in support, but let me quote only one relating to a most generous soul from ancient Arabia. His name was Hatim Tai. He gained reputation as the most generous person of his time. Once someone questioned him, 'Have you come across anyone more generous than yourself?'

'Yes, I have,' replied Hatim Tai. When he was asked to name the person, Hatim Tai narrated the following story:

I had been travelling in the desert when I came across a tent. Inside it was an old lady while behind the tent there was a goat tied to a post. When the old lady saw me, she approached me and held the reigns of my horse so that I could dismount. A little later, her son arrived and was immensely pleased to have me as their guest. The old lady said to him, "Commence the preparations to entertain our guest. Go and slaughter the goat and prepare some food."

The son said, "First, I shall go and collect some firewood." But the old lady interrupted him and said, "Going out into the desert to bring firewood will take a lot of time; our guest would have to remain hungry for a long time, and this would be contrary to our social etiquette."

So the son, breaking the only two lances that he possessed, slaughtered the goat, prepared the food and served it to me. When I investigated their living condition, I realized that the goat had been their only possession and despite this, they had slaughtered it for me. I said to the old lady, "Do you recognize me?" When she replied in the negative, I said, "I am Hatim Tai. You must come with me to my tribe so that I can entertain you and shower you with gifts and presents!"

The old lady said, "Neither do we seek any reward from our guests nor do we sell bread for money." She refused to accept anything from me. Witnessing this generosity, I recognized that they were far more generous and munificent than me."

Today, generosity is taken as *giving out of your surpluses*. Giving all that you have discarded is no giving. Giving what you cannot afford to lose is giving. That is generosity. Likewise, giving for gaining fame is no generosity.

True Generosity

How mean am I when Life gives me gold and I give you silver, and yet I deem myself generous!
—Kahlil Gibran, *The Greatest Works of Kahlil Gibran*

Corporate social responsibility is carried out with a big fanfare! When the corporate pharaohs pay an insignificant amount from their huge profits, it becomes the big news in media. When fame becomes aim, the spirit of generosity is lost.

In the olden days, *guests* were considered as God's gift—serving them was like serving God. No one can feed guests—it is God who feeds them through you. I have seen many houses prospering when they espoused hospitality. I have seen the same household falling down when they withdrew hospitality. This *spiritual equation* cannot be explained through mathematics.

If you want to measure the health of any household, find out how many guests visited that house during the last month.

If you want to make life happy, be generous to others. When needy persons come to your door, thank God for sending them and do not let them return without giving some charity.

The great Sufi, Kahlil Gibran, says: 'Generosity is not in giving me that which I need more than you do, but it is in giving me that which you need more than I do.' I wish leaders understand this wisdom and change the profile of leadership. Change of heart in leadership can change the world.

If you judge people, you have no time to love them.

—Mother Teresa

9

Managing 'Conflicting Perspectives'

Was the love of Judas' mother for her son less than the love of Mary for Jesus?
—Kahlil Gibran, *The Greatest Works of Kahlil Gibran*

I start with a Zen story to explain the art of developing a holistic perception, and then shall share the techniques for managing the conflicting perspectives.

In ancient China, on top of Mount Ping stood a temple, where enlightened master, Hawan dwelled. Lao-li was one of his disciples who was struggling to attain enlightenment. Once, while he was meditating, a falling cherry blossom said to his heart, 'I can no longer fight my destiny.' Lao-li gave up his hope of enlightenment and informed his master of his decision to go back home. His great Zen master agreed. 'Tomorrow, I will join you on your journey down the mountain,' he told Lao-li.

The next morning before their descent, the great master looked out into the vastness surrounding the mountain peak and asked, 'Tell me, Lao-li, what do you see?'

'Master, I see the sun beginning to rise just below the horizon, meandering hills and mountains that go on for miles, and couched in the valley below, a lake and an old town,' said Lao-li.

The master listened to Lao-li's response. He smiled, and then they took the first step of their descent. On reaching the foot of the mountain, again Hawan asked Lao-li to tell him what he saw.

'Great wise one, in the distance I see the roosters as they run around barns, cows asleep in sprouting meadows, old men and women basking in the later afternoon sun, and children romping by a brook.' The master remained silent. They continued to walk until they reached the gate of the town.

They sat under an old tree. 'What did you learn today Lao-li?' asked the master. 'Perhaps this the last bit of wisdom I will impart to you.' Silence was Lao-li's response.

At last, after a long silence, the master continued, 'The road to enlightenment is like the journey down the mountain. It comes only to those who realize that what one sees at the top of the mountain is not what one sees at the bottom. Without this wisdom, we close our capacity to grow and improve. But with wisdom, Lao-li, there comes an awakening. We recognize that above one sees only so much—which, in turn, is not much at all. This is wisdom that opens our minds to improvement, knocks down prejudices, and teaches us to respect what at first we cannot view. Never forget this last lesson, Lao-li—what you cannot see can be seen from a different part of the mountain.'

Understanding a holistic pattern is of great significance in management. Lack of holistic understanding creates problems in management. What the lower rung workers see the issues at the bottom of the pyramid are not well understood by the top management, not sometimes but many a time. Likewise, the problems faced by the top management owing to finance deficiencies, the changing business trends, changing patterns of demand and supply of the products or services are not well appreciated by the lower rung workers and supervisors. Lack of holistic perception is one of the major causes of industrial unrest and stirs.

The phrase 'Tall see the farthest' does not mean that the people of taller heights can see farther than those who are shorter in height. It refers to the inner eye, which helps foresee that others fail to see. People who understand their present and can foresee the futuristic trends or patterns become visionary. In leadership we call them visionary leaders. Those who develop better perception can develop better perspective. Perspectives change with perception. It is *perception* that creates *perspective*.

Perspectives vary from person to person. Everyone holds a different perspective about different things and many a time, different people hold different perspectives about the same thing. Amusingly, one's own perspective changes with the passage of time.

The famous quotation of Shakespeare, 'Fair is foul and foul is fair', explains the truth about the variety of perspectives. What we call *subjectivity* is nothing but the differing perspectives of people.

A Sufi judge was known for his wisdom. Once, two persons approached his court. One charged the other saying that he had beaten him although there was no cause or provocation from his side. After listening to his statement carefully, the Sufi judge said: 'You are right.' On hearing this, the accused could not keep quiet. He made a loud protest saying, 'Sir, you have not even heard my statement and told this guy that he is right.'

> ### I Am Right; You Are Wrong
>
> Is there a greater fault than be conscious of other person's fault?
> Strange that we all defend our wrongs with more vigour than we do our rights!
> —Kahlil Gibran, *The Greatest Works of Kahlil Gibran*

The Sufi judge turned his face towards him and said: 'You are right.' Upon this the munshi—the guy who was noting down the proceedings for the purpose of maintaining the court's records—made a mild protest by saying, 'Sir, you tell each of them that he is right. I don't know how to record your judgment. I am confused!' The Sufi judge now looked at him and nodded his head saying, 'You are right!' Everyone is right in his or her perception.

Leaders must develop wisdom and attain insight to understand and see other's way of understanding. Judas might be a sinner in the eye of the world, but for her mother he was most loveable person. There is no other way to understand a person save through the route of heart. Once one creates the heart of Judas' mother, he or she can discover Judas' mother's love for Judas.

> **Fruit-bearing Trees Receive the Stones!**
>
> Nightingales are put in the cages because their songs give pleasure. Whoever heard of keeping a crow in the cage?
> —Jelaluddin Rumi, *RUMI Daylight—A Daybook of Spiritual Guidance*

Ordinary leaders, not the great ones, get offended when someone criticises them. Great personalities have greater tolerance and do not get perturbed. Thousands of articles were written against Albert Einstein when he came up with his famous Quantum Theory. He smiled and said, 'Had I been really wrong, I couldn't have attracted 1000 genius to write against me.' Only fruit-bearing trees receive the stones. Have you ever seen a boy throwing stones on the oak tree?

In my book *Watch your Ladder*, I had mentioned the one mistake that most of us make: *We try to look at others' perceptions through our perception.* This way we become judgemental. We call the others' way of thinking right or wrong, keeping our way of thinking in mind.

Most of the problems in any society arise due to differing perceptions. Perceptions do differ. Even if they match, they seldom match perfectly. If you want to understand a person, try to understand his way of understanding of a particular thing, viewpoint or situation. You still have the right to agree or differ with him but the advantage now is that you will understand why he thought of a particular thing in a particular manner. Understanding another's perception does not impose any condition on us to agree with him.

Therefore, never say, 'I don't agree with you.' Instead, say, 'I hold a different perception.' The former hurts; the latter conveys soberly the same meaning. Is your purpose to hurt or to convey?

When two persons hold two different perceptions, there still exists a small space of *common understanding*. If you want to sell your viewpoint to others, do not start with the differences but begin with the common ground of understanding. Unfortunately, most of the time, many of us begin the dialogue by keeping the focus on differences while ignoring the *common ground of understanding* (Figure 9.1).

Leaders with wisdom always start their viewpoint, keeping in focus the *common ground of understanding*. Once you start with the *common ground of understanding*, other person becomes receptive. The space of *common ground of understanding* gradually enlarges once the rapport is built and both try to understand other's point of view with an open mind. This technique yields good results (Figure 9.2).

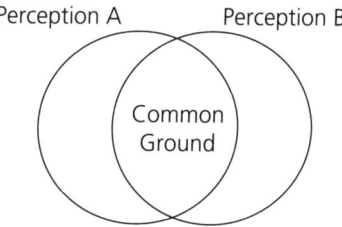

FIGURE 9.1

Locate a *Common Ground* to Understand Others' Perception

Source: Moid Siddiqui.

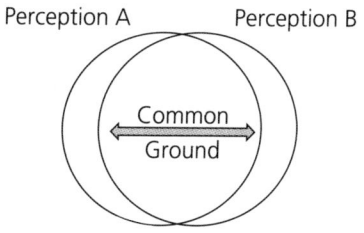

FIGURE 9.2

Increasing Space of '*Common* Understanding'

Source: Moid Siddiqui.

I have given a name to this technique: Creating Agreement in Disagreement. I was inspired in developing this technique from Mark Antony's speech in Shakespeare's famous drama *Julius Caesar*.

Recall, after Brutus and his accomplices murdered Julius Caesar, Mark Antony appears at the church ground. He is already a man distrusted by the conspirators for his friendship with Caesar. Brutus lets him speak at Caesar's funeral but only after he (Brutus—a great orator in his own right) has spoken first to 'show the reason of our Caesar's death'. Brutus makes it clear that Mark Antony may speak whatever good he wishes of Caesar so long as he speaks no ill of the conspirators. The entire crowd was motivated against Julius Caesar by the conspirators' speeches, which justified the murder of Caesar for the sake of country and countrymen. The crowd was now emotionally charged up against Caesar and it was in this *hostile* situation that Mark Antony begins his famous speech:

Friends, Romans, countrymen, lend me your ears: I come to bury Caesar, not to praise him. The evil that men do lives after them. The good is oft interred with their bones. So let it be with Caesar. The noble Brutus has told you Caesar was ambitious. If it were so, it was a grievous fault, and grievously hath Caesar answered it.

Here, under leave of Brutus and the rest—for Brutus is an honourable man; so are they all, all honourable men—come I to speak in Caesar's funeral. He was my friend, faithful and just to me.

But Brutus says he was ambitious, and Brutus is an honourable man. He hath brought many captives home to Rome whose ransoms did the general coffers fill. Did this in Caesar seem ambitious? When that the poor have cried, Caesar hath wept. Ambition should be made of sterner stuff.

Yet, Brutus says he was ambitious, and Brutus is an honourable man.

You all did see that on the Lupercal I thrice presented him a kingly crown, which he did thrice refuse. Was this ambition? Yet Brutus says he was ambitious, and, sure he is an honourable man.

I speak not to disprove what Brutus spoke. But here I am to speak what I do know. You all did love him once, not without cause. What cause withholds you, then, to mourn for him? Oh, Judgment, thou are fled to brutish beasts, and men have lost their reason.

Bear with me: My heart is in the coffin there with Caesar, and I must pause till it comes back to me …

Even though Antony never directly calls the conspirators traitors, he repeatedly calls them 'honourable' in a sarcastic manner so that the crowd is able to understand. He starts with what Brutus and his accomplices had claimed—they killed Julius Caesar as he had become too ambitious. Then he changes the gear and starts citing the incidents Caesar's refusal to the crown three times. This way he cleverly refutes the conspirators' main cause for killing Caesar. He reminds them of Caesar's kindness and love for all, humanising Caesar as innocent. Next he teases them with 'Caesar's Will', not disclosing its contents. When the masses demand, he reveals Caesar's *gift* to the citizens. Finally, Marc Antony leaves them with the question: *Was there ever a greater one than Caesar?* This last punch line was so powerful that the crowd fully turns hostile.

Technique of Creating Agreement in Disagreement: *First, make the person(s) 'receptive' by touching the points of common understanding, and then gradually, not at once, move towards the counterpoint. Such a move creates a tremendous impact on others.*

Life-success lies in understanding others' perceptions and selling your viewpoint in such a subtle manner that others are not hurt. Now I share another technique, what Gold Ratt, the author of famous book *The Goal*, has devised. It is a beautiful technique to resolve the disputes that arise owing to conflicting perspectives.

Technique of *Building a Cloud*: The phrase 'A silver lining behind the dark clouds' conveys the ray of hope. A cloud is an elegant graphical means of displaying and solving an apparent conflict or dilemma between two persons. *Building a cloud* has become a metaphor—a technique to resolve differences. *Cloud building* technique entails two important aspects. First, go deep and locate the roots of the conflict. Second, find a solution by aligning the (apparent) opposite objectives with a win-win approach.

Problems exist because people feel they exist. People have the tendency to keep focus on problems and not on the solutions. When you keep focus on the conflicting perspectives, in fact you are keeping focus on problem. But when you focus on the *common ground of understanding*, you become the part of solution. You get what you focus on!

In nature there are no problems—there are only patterns. Likewise, clouds may acquire many patterns, yet each pattern is unique in itself. Clouds make patterns effortlessly. The pattern goes on changing constantly. Each pattern looks beautiful. You can also create a beautiful pattern in your life. Let me explain the technique of *building a cloud* through a live situation:

When Gold Ratt, author of the famous book—The Goal, returns home tired and spent, he finds his wife and daughter arguing heatedly. When he asks his wife, she refuses to tell him the cause and says he had better ask his beloved daughter. On hearing this, his daughter gets angry and says, "Mom always treats me like a small baby." Gold Ratt does not get any clue from this statement. So, he once again asks his wife to tell him the entire story.

Gold Ratt's wife then shares with him the news that their daughter wants to go for a late-night dance and dinner party. When she did not agree to her demand, she was very annoyed and started arguing with her. Now Gold Ratt turns to his daughter and asks her to tell him her side of the story. She confirms that she wants to go for a dinner party but her mother is not allowing her only because she still treats her as a baby. She has entered her teens and she does not want to be ridiculed by her friends; they would tease her if she told them that her mother has not permitted her to attend the dance and dinner party. She makes it clear that it is a question of her image. She no more wants to be recognized as a small girl—she is now a teenager and ready to enter adulthood.

Gold Ratt is now in a dilemma. Whom to support? If he supports his wife, who has a genuine cause for the denial, the daughter will turn rebellious. In case he supports his daughter, he will be spoiling her by agreeing to what he himself does not like. Besides, he will also antagonize his wife and the situation would only worsen!

The situation was quite delicate. Gold Ratt didn't know how to resolve the issue. At this juncture he decides to 'Build a Cloud'. He makes the analysis and tries to understand the point of worry of his wife and the point of anxiety of his daughter. His wife was worried for the 'safety' of her daughter and the anxiety of his daughter was for her 'image' before her friends. If she did not attend the dance and dinner party they would tease her by calling her, 'Baby'.

Once Gold Ratt understands these two crucial aspects from their different perspectives, it becomes easy for him to 'Build the Cloud'.

"When will the party end?" Gold Ratt asks his daughter.

"I don't know, when!" She shrugs her shoulders. "It can be mid-night or beyond."

"How you will return home?" Gold Ratt asks another question, ignoring her arrogance and making her feel his concern.

"Tom says he will drop me on his bike."

"Drinks will be served before dinner?" Gold Ratt shoots another question.

"I don't drink, you know it well Dad," replies the daughter, in a milder tone.

"But Tom will drink."

"Yes," she says, truthfully.

"How safe will you be on the bike driven by a person who is drunk?"

His daughter wants to say something, but words refuse to come to her tongue. As an expert 'Cloud Builder', Gold Ratt knows this is the right time to strike.

"Look, you are going to the party. Your Mom will not stop you." Gold Ratt makes this commitment knowing fully well that his wife will not like this. But he also knows that she will feel consoled on hearing what he is going to say next.

"You are going to the party and coming back with me, not with Tom," says Gold Ratt, in a decisive and commanding voice.

"But...," the girl fumbled.

"I know what you are thinking. I will drop you a few yards away from your venue—your friends will not know that I have dropped you. Don't bother, you will retain your 'teen image'," assures Gold Ratt.

The girl keeps silent, as she has no excuse to offer.

"I will wait in the car, away from your dinner place, till midnight or beyond. As your father, it is a small price that I am willing to pay for your safety," says Gold Ratt, looking deep into her eyes.

"No Dad, you need not wait that long. I shall come back at thirty minutes past ten, even if the party is not finished. I assure you Dad," replies the girl, with tears in her eyes. Gold Ratt comes forward and gives her a big hug. The girl, then turns towards her mother and says, "Sorry Mom—I hurt you." She gets a passionate hug from her mother. The conflict was resolved with a win-win solution.

In life, there occur many conflicts, owing to conflicting perspectives. There is a good method to resolve a conflict—change the perspective by following two steps: (a) First find out the root cause, (b) then look for the solution with *win-win* approach.

Each conflict hides a solution at its deepest level. A Sufi sees the conflict with a different perspective. 'A disagreement is the shortest cut between two minds,' says Kahlil Gibran.[1] This gives up the hope that disagreement can be changed into agreement. Disagreement is nothing but differing perspectives. Once the right perspective is created, disagreement disappears.

A positive perspective creates harmony and coherence—a negative perspective leads to disharmony and chaos. Harmony makes things grow—disharmony creates decadence. The role of a good leader is to create harmony. If he leads people by creating disharmony following the policy of *divide and rule*, then he is not a

[1] Kahlil Gibran, *The Greatest Works of Kahlil Gibran.*

leader but a *misleader*. Today many *misleaders* are respected because people do not understand the real characteristics of leadership or the levels of leadership-consciousness!

Great leaders always see the Big Picture by developing a holistic pattern. Managing conflicting perspectives is an art that every leader must master.

To completely trust in God is to be like a child who knows deeply that even if he does not call for the mother, the mother is totally aware of his condition and is looking after him.

—*Imam al Ghazali*

10

DEVELOP A HEART THAT CAN TRUST

Faith is a knowledge within the heart, beyond the reach of proof.
—KAHLIL GIBRAN, *THE GREATEST WORKS OF KAHLIL GIBRAN*

Preaching and rendering sermons on *trust* is easy but demonstrating trust in practice is not that easy. Though it may appear an insignificant instance to many, it is one of most memorable incidents of my life.

The year was 1990. *Corporate promotions* was one of the tasks assigned to me. I was reporting to H.R. Alva, Director (Personnel). I rendered my assistance to him by organising interviews of senior executives at 25 factories at different locations. I got the promotion proceedings computerised and made all the necessary arrangements that the new career growth policy required. Since I was also one of the candidates, I wanted to distance myself from the process but my boss, H.R. Alva, Director (Personnel), felt otherwise. After each day of interviews, he handed over the selection proceedings to me.

At the end of the day on which I was interviewed, I was amazingly surprised—he once again gave the proceedings to me for custody. I took them in my shaking hands. But the boss had given those confidential papers fully trusting me. And, believe me, I reciprocated that trust—I never glanced through the selection proceedings. I came to know of my promotion only when the orders were issued to the successful executives. This simple gesture of trust by my boss is so deeply engraved in my mind that I can never forget. *Trust begets trust* is not merely a phrase, I realised.

Some people consider *faith* as the seed of *trust*. Some believe, *it is trust through which you develop faith*. In fact, *trust* and *faith* are two faces of the same coin. Once you have faith in someone, you begin trusting him. Once you start trusting, your faith solidifies. Contrarily, once mistrust enters your heart about somebody, you lose faith in him. 'I don't have any faith in you; I no more trust you,' is the common dialogue that we hear many times from people with broken hearts.

This is the story of a man who rolled down from a snow-clad mountain in the dead of the night. While sliding down into the deep valley, he somehow found a long tree-root, which he could hold. Now he was hovering in the air. It was pitch dark and he could not see anything. The bone-biting cold and the fear of death by falling into the gorge below made him remember God. We remember God only when we are in trouble! God also knows our nature well. He knows our selfish nature and ungratefulness to Him.

"Do you really trust me?" asked God

"Yes, I fully trust you," replied the man.

"Then listen to my words carefully and do as I say," God commanded and the man, who was seeing his death even in the darkness, promised to obey.

"Say, 'Oh God, I trust you'," God said. The man repeated what God asked him to say.

"Good!" God was pleased. "Now, loosen your grip and leave the root that you are holding."

"No, God!" cried the man, fearing his death. "If I loosen my grip, I will fall into the deep valley." God told him to let go of the root many times but the man did not loosen his grip for fear of a great fall to death. Yet each time God asked, "Do you trust Me?", the man replied in affirmation.

In the morning, people of the valley came and they were surprised to see a frozen dead body hanging just one foot above the ground level. Had the man really trusted God and let go of the root, he would have saved his life.

God can get you anything in Life and make you anything you want to be. The secret is to 'Trust Him'!

Trusting God is trusting Life. Life without God becomes meaningless. Life is the created thing; it is not the Creator per se! It is not the created thing that deserves reverence; it is the Creator whom we should revere. How can you revere one unless you trust Him and acknowledge His existence? So, trust God—revere Him, and you will win the trust of life. Trusting God and His wisdom warrants a total unconditional surrender to His Will; this trust comes not through words but through your belief, actions and deeds. And the actions and deeds will be meaningless in the absence of sincerity and earnestness. 'Actions are merely propped-up shapes,' observes Ibn Ata'llah, a Sufi, 'Their life-breath is the presence of the secret of *sincerity* in them.' Apple-polishing does not give you results—your deeds must flow from the sincerity of your heart.

Trust begins with love; mistrust with hatred. Develop a loving heart. Fill your heart with love. True trust begins with love. One can hate and trust simultaneously, but that is not genuine trust. Trust must flow from the depth of your heart, where love resides. True love dwells in the deepness of the heart. Trusting

> **Unshaken Faith**
>
> O God! If I worship You for fear of Hell, burn me in Hell, and if I worship You in hope of Paradise, exclude me from Paradise. But if I worship You for Your Own sake, grudge me not Your everlasting Beauty.
>
> —Rabia of Basra (a female Sufi)

someone out of fear is no trust. Trust must flow from love, not from fear.

People say, 'We love you, we trust your words ...' Such shallow words, which are uttered from habit by your tongue, are not the true reflection of your real feelings. A shaken faith or half-hearted belief is incapable of turning events into miracles.

People went to a saint and requested him to offer prayers for rain, as there was a drought. The saint asked the villagers to assemble in the open ground in front of the temple. When all the villagers assembled, the saint offered his prayers. No miracle happened. No black clouds came and so it did not rain. The villagers were very angry. The leader came forward and accused the saint of shaking their faith in prayers.

"Did you really have faith in me and my prayers?" asked the saint.

"Yes," said the man.

"Did you really believe that my prayers would make rain clouds appear and cause showers?" the saint asked, once again.

"Yes," the man said, in disgust.

"Then why didn't you or anyone in the crowd carry umbrellas?"

The villagers understood the subtle message of the saint. They felt sorry for their half-hearted faith in the saint's prayers.

Miracles happen with faith, not with shallow prayers. Prayers without faith in them are incapable of playing miracles. Since you trust, miracles take place. I remember a dialogue of a famous Hindi film *Guide*. In a drought-stricken village, when the actor Dev Anand, the hero of the film *Guide*, observes fast at the request of the villagers and was about to die of hunger, a journalist asks him, 'Do you really believe that your fast will get the showers?' He gives a very powerful reply: 'This is the faith of the villagers and I have full faith in their faith.' No wonder, a miracle takes place and the villagers get heavy showers.

Not only develop a heart that can trust, but also create a culture of trust in your organisation. The culture of trust can be created only when you follow the principle *Zero Tolerance for Mistrust*.

Ricardo Semler, an entrepreneur of Brazil (author of *Maverick*), uniquely turned around his company SEMCO by following a simple principle—*Zero Tolerance for Mistrust*. He is a maverick who followed certain practices, which were never practiced earlier by any other CEO.

> ### Zero Tolerance to Mistrust
>
> I would rather have a few theft once in a while than condemn everyone to a system based on **Mistrust**. Have Thefts and Time-card cheating increased or decreased? I don't know and I don't care! It's not worth it to me to have a company at which you don't trust the people with whom you work!
>
> —Ricardo Semler CEO, SEMCO, *Maverick*

Once, Ricardo received an anonymous letter against two of his executives who had placed orders for prodders worth more than $500,000 with the supplier. 'But we had embarked on a new era of trust at SEMCO and it seemed consistent with that spirit to discount accusations that were not accompanied by solid evidence or even the accuser's name,' writes Ricardo. Instead of investigating the actions of the executives, Ricardo decided to investigate the anonymous complainant with a clear mind. 'If the allegations were false then we certainly did not want such a person working for us. If they were true, we should take the appropriate action, but we also wanted to know why such an underhand method of exposure was necessary.' Ricardo never wanted to encourage anonymous letters; these reflect a sign of lack of trust and lack of courage on the part of the sender. More surprisingly, he did not take action against the defaulting executives but took action against those who were party to the authorship of that anonymous letter. 'So the two executives were exonerated and the accusers were dismissed. Only then did everyone come to know about the case,' claims Ricardo. With this action, he made it loud and clear that when he said *Zero tolerance for Mistrust*, he meant it. One may ridicule his action but his surgery created a miracle and helped build a *culture of openness* where people were encouraged to come forward and share openly their views—good or bad—about the organisation but not through anonymity, which is a sign of cowardice.

It takes time to build the *culture of trust*. Trust is not built with words. Trust is built by *see-able* actions. In a lighter vein, let me share a twisted anecdote about Hitler. It appears that Adolph Hitler had attended a session in International School of Business Management on the theme 'Trust and Faith in Life'. On his return, he called a meeting of his military commanders and announced that he was a changed person with a noble soul. He declared that he had adopted the policy of openness to build the bonds of strong relationships through *trust* and *faith*. Therefore, he asked his commanders to share their mind frankly and without fear. Trusting his words, one commander boldly criticised some his dictatorial policies. To their great surprise, they found Hitler very receptive and sincere to such negative feedback. He took each word with humility and a soothing smile on his face. Everyone was wonderstruck on the miraculous change of heart. 'Since the suggestion given by honourable commander is very important, I want to discuss this in detail.' Then he invited the commander to his secret chamber.

Both went inside in a friendly manner. After some time, only Hitler came out.

'Leadership is all about *trust* and *faith*,' says the former Military Commander of the US, Collin Powel. 'Great leaders are trustworthy. Why would anyone follow you for the uphill tasks, giving their best, sometimes even risking their lives?' Trust implies

Trust and Integrity

I look for three things in hiring people. The first is *Personal Integrity*, the second is *Intelligence* and the third is a high *Energy Level*.

But if you don't have the first, the second two don't matter.

—Warren Buffett

accountability, predictability, reliability, and above all integrity. *Faith* and *trust* keep the organisation humming. Trust is the glue that maintains organisational integrity. You cannot manage a company without integrity. You cannot have success without trust. Building trust is the crucial success factor of business management as well as personal life, though it scarcely exists in today's world.

Trust and faith are not built through words, they are built through actions—it takes time to *grow* with trust. You cannot grow apples by sowing the seeds of a jackfruit. You cannot expect to build trust by mistrusting others. Let me quote a true incident. I was working in HMT—a premier public sector organisation in India. Whenever I walked through the corridor to meet the Chief of Administration, I would see a *steel tumbler* chained to the water cooler. I pleaded many times with my colleague that this indicates lack of trust, which is not good for the spiritual health of the organisation. He always laughed at my views saying that he had already lost six tumblers and he was in no mood to lose a seventh. My argument was that let us lose another one dozen tumblers yet not lose our heart in building up trust. This, however, was not at all acceptable to him. I confess, I failed in convincing him and the tumbler remained chained to the water-cooling machine.

I was so disturbed with the sight of that *chained steel tumbler* that sometimes it used to haunt me in my dreams. With all my trust in *trust* and all my faith in *faith*, I could not manage to *unleash* the steel tumbler.

During those days, I had visited the complex of Verifone, a multinational organisation in Bangalore. My colleague manager took me to her staff canteen. As we returned, I found a big glass jar on the table near the exit. 'Honesty Jar' was boldly inscribed

The Issue of This Decade

Technique and Technology are important, but adding Trust is the issue of the decade.

—Tom Peters

on it. Obviously, I was keen to know from the Verifone manager all about that *Honesty Jar*. She explained that they did not have a system of canteen coupons. Prices were displayed and employees were supposed to put the money in the Honesty Jar as per what they had consumed. 'You must be in trouble at the end of the day!' I said, with a mischievous smile. 'You are right,' she said, agreeing with me but in the same breath she added, 'But not the kind of *trouble* you are thinking of in your mind.' Then she explained that her trouble was that every day she found an excess amount and she just did not know what to do with that extra money. She then explained that since the company had demonstrated its ability in building trust, the employees were reciprocating with more sincerity and honesty. Each employee thought that if even one employee demonstrated dishonesty, the amount in the Honesty Jar would fall short. So to overcome this, some of the employees put extra money in the jar so that the end-result would reflect *honouring the trust*.

The above experiment gave the opposite result than that in the famous *Milk Pot* anecdote:

A King, in order to check the trustworthiness of his people, asked every citizen to bring a mug full of milk to be poured into a huge pot. Each citizen thought to himself, "Surely others are going to bring pure milk. So why should I not pour water into the pot? It will hardly make any difference and the King will never know". When everyone had poured the contents of their mug into the hug pot, the King came to see the milk in the big collection pot. To his surprise he found no milk, only water! When you create an environment of mistrust, all controls fail and what you get is only mistrust.

Like a fruit juicer, life pours out what you feed into it. You cannot blame the juicer if you get sour fruit juice. But we always blame life for our mistakes.

Here I must caution and make it clear that trust is different from gullibility—blind trust. Blind trust is foolish. If you share your life secrets or company secrets with everyone trusting everyone blindly, surely you will be in trouble. 'If you reveal your secrets to the wind,' says Kahlil Gibran, 'you should not blame the wind for revealing them to the trees'.[1] One must understand clearly the difference between *trust* and *gullibility*. It is dangerous to trust everyone; it is most dangerous not to trust anyone. Both are bad. When I say *trust*, I mean *smart trust*.

There is yet another dimension of *trust*. It is *credibility*. Trust and credibility are not one and the same, though we use these two words as two sides of a coin that always go along together. While at times trust brings credibility, there are occasions when credibility results in trust. Though they are both offspring of *faith*, yet there is a stark difference between *trust* and *credibility*.

To explain *credibility*, I am tempted to narrate an anecdote relating to Mulla Nasrudin, a Sufi, who was known to grant wisdom to people through his foolhardiness.

> *Mull Nasrudin struck up a conversation with a stranger:*
>
> *"Ar one point," he asked, "So how's business?"*
>
> *"Great," the stranger replied, wondering why an unknown person was asking such question!*
>
> *"Then, can I borrow ten dirhams?"*
>
> *"No. I don't know you well enough to lend you money."*
>
> *"That's strange," replied Nasrudin. "Where I used to live, people wouldn't lend me money because they knew me; and now that I've moved here, people won't lend me money because they don't know me!"*

Humour apart, while you could choose to trust someone, or not, you really don't have any direct say on *your own credibility*—others do. You may make efforts to earn trust but it doesn't automatically get you credibility. That seal of credibility remains in others' hands. So, simply said, *it is merely through continuous trust that you can foster (not enforce) credibility*.

---

[1] Kahlil Gibran, *The Greatest Works of Khalil Gibran.*

Trust begets trust and mistrust creates mistrust. Through trust you can win the heart of God, let alone the hearts of people!

Leadership is all about *trust and credibility*. Great leaders are trustworthy. They trust their people and have faith in their competencies and capabilities. They win their hearts creating credibility for your leadership. *Trust* and *credibility* relate to higher levels of leadership-consciousness. Only when you develop a trusting heart, will you be trusted and given credibility.

Win the hearts of your people by creating credibility. Then, you will be a witness to many a miracle in *personal life* as well as in *corporate life*!

It was pride that changed angels into devils; it is humility that makes men as angels.

—*Saint Augustine*

11

MARINATE LEADERSHIP IN HUMILITY

When God threw me, a pebble, into this wondrous lake I disturbed its surface
with countless circles. But when I reached the depth, I became still.
—KAHLIL GIBRAN, *THE GREATEST WORKS OF KAHLIL GIBRAN*

Humility is the sign of ripen sagacity. It lies at the deepest layer of wisdom. Only a few can reach such depth.

I recall and reiterate an incident.

It was a festive occasion at IIM, Bangalore. The tailor-made programme for the technologists was being inaugurated. I was invited as a member to the advisory board on this new venture for technologists. I was keenly involved in this mission.

The chief guest, for some reason, could not make it. The responsibly of the keynote address was shifted to another speaker. Obviously, the audience did not expect much from the surrogate speaker. This speaker spoke amazingly well, punctuating his speech with humility. I was deeply impressed.

On my return, I decided to write a letter to him expressing my wholehearted appreciation and sharing some of my thoughts. I wrote that his was one of the rare speeches I had heard. I expected a warm and quick response. Days, weeks and months passed. I did not get the response. When all hopes of getting a reply withered away, like a fresh breeze came these humble words in print to convince me that the beauty that I had found in his verbal thoughts equally persisted in his aesthetic prose. His humble words whizzed the hex.

> *I took sometime to reply because it is not easy to respond to a letter so rich in ideas and concepts. With people of erudition—poets, playwrights, men of letters like you in the audience, I should be careful in what I speak. The noble ears like yours always hear only good and for that reason my simple talk appeared so great to you. Thanks.*

Humility Is Akin to Greatness

The good-to-great leaders never wanted to become larger-than-life heroes. They never aspired to be put on a pedestal or become unreachable icons. They were seemingly ordinary people quietly producing extra-ordinary results.

—Jim Collin,
Good to Great

Wow! What a great leader with serenity, modesty and humility! I cannot forget the gesture of humility of the great leader. I was myself sobered with his humility. He had so beautifully assigned his memorable talk to the high quality of the audience. Giving wholesome credit to others needs a large heart—only great people can do.

Humility is a great gift of God. Leaders with humility scale greater heights. They speak less; act more. One quality of humble leaders is that they never raise their voice, yet their words carry force. 'Raise your words, not the voice,' suggests Rumi. 'It is rain that grows flowers, not the thunder.' People of wisdom speak less and act more. 'In silence there is eloquence,' says Rumi.[1]

A leader who travels from his *head* to *heart* acquires humility. *Humility, tranquillity, dignity* and *patience* are four major components

[1] Jelaluddin Rumi, *RUMI Daylight—A Daybook of Spiritual Guidance.*

of greatness. When you are immature, you try to create ripples. When you attain maturity, you become a *mountain's lake*—silent, serene and peaceful. 'No one can see one's reflection in the running water. It is only in still water that one can see,' writes Lao Tzu in his famous book *Tao Te Ching*. It takes time to acquire greatness—humility comes with maturity in leadership. A leader without humility can never command respect from his people.

What Lao Tzu—the Old Master—envisaged in his famous book *Tao Te Ching* has become the profile of today's leadership. One of the traits of the fifth level of leadership is personal humility added with professional will of the leader. Though I do not believe in gradation in terms of numbers, yet I cannot ignore the way modern mavens measure the quality of leadership. Greatness in leadership lies in compelling modesty, shunning public adulation, negation of boastfulness, quiet and calm nature. Such great leaders are not only humble but also large-hearted. They look out the window, not in the mirror, to give credit for the success of the company. They look in the mirror, not out the windows, to own responsibility for poor results.

Humility is one of the best attributes of leadership. Humility is the sign of spirituality. It is also the sign of wisdom and deeper level of consciousness. 'Be humble,' says the Bhagvad Gita, 'be harmless, have no pretensions, be upright, forbearing, serve in true obedience.' A good leader gives his people the pleasant feeling that they have accomplished the tasks by themselves.

Humility—The Sign of Greatness

A sense of humility is a quality I have observed in every leader who I have deeply admired. I have seen Winston Churchill with humble tears of gratitude on his cheeks as he thanked the people for their help to Britain and the Allied cause. My own conviction is that every leader should have enough humility to accept publicly, the responsibility for the mistakes of the subordinates he has himself selected and, likewise, to give them credit publicly for their triumphs.

—Dwight Eisenhower (former President of the US)

Great leaders stay in the background and watch things move in the right direction. They let their people steal their ideas and give credit to them. They do it so subtly that his people do not have any feeling of guilt.

Plato wrote in the 4th century BC: 'Those having torches will pass them on to others.' Leaders with deeper consciousness do this with all humility. That is greatness in leadership!

The great irony is that most leaders possess diagonally opposite profile. Instead of personal humility, they possess personal ambition, which often drives them towards building their own *power centres*. Unfortunately the selection boards, in most of cases, look for hiring a larger-than-life, egocentric leaders misconstruing that they would lead people and organisation towards excellence. Many times selections are made on their appearance. One of the most damaging trends today is the tendency to select dazzling, celebrity leaders for the positions of board of directors and CEOs of companies. It is a great agony that humility and sagacity is not given any credit in such selections. Why? It is because the selectors measure the track record in numbers not in quality.

Appearances are deceptive sometimes. We tend to always judge people by their outer appearance, which can be very misleading. As mentioned, Mulla Nasrudin was a Sufi. Sufis do not bother for their external self; they work on their inner self. Once he went to the palace for a feast-day—but when the servants noticed his ragged clothes, they paid him no attention and offered him no food. And so, Nasrudin went back to his house, put on his most extravagant clothing, and returned to the palace, where this time he was treated like royalty, and had numerous dishes placed in front of him. Nasrudin then proceeded to take handfuls of food and pour and rubbing them into his clothing—causing another guest to ask, 'What in the world are you doing?' 'Oh, I am just feeding my clothing first,' was the reply. 'After all, they are what got me this food!'

If you want to understand a person, reach him through the route of heart. Humility is like an ocean—the greatness lies in its tranquillity. 'Only when you drink from the river of silence shall you indeed sing,' says Kahlil Gibran. 'And when you have reached the mountain top, then you shall begin to climb.' Humility is the sign of greatness! Marinate your leadership in humility, and see what difference it makes!

Humble leaders do not think themselves less; they only think less about themselves.

The life we live is an expression of the choices we make.

—*Laurie Buchanan*

12

LAW OF ENERGY RESPONSE

We often borrow from our tomorrows to pay debts to our yesterday.
—KAHLIL GIBRAN, *THE GREATEST WORKS OF KAHLIL GIBRAN*

We live in consequences—as we sow, so we reap. The Taoist Universal Law of Energy Response is law of karma without rebirth. You reap the harvest of your deeds in this very lifetime, or in the eternal life, after death. Recompenses follow our actions as the shadow follows the substance.

I begin this chapter with a short anecdote—simple but quite meaningful.

A woman baked bread for members of the family and an extra one for a hungry passer by. She kept the extra bread on the windowsill, for whosoever would take it away. Every day a hunchback came and took away the bread. Instead of expressing gratitude, he muttered the following words as he went his way: "The evil you do remains with you; the good you do, comes back to you!" This went on, day after day.

Every day, the hunchback came, picked up the bread and uttered the words: "The evil you do, remains with you; the good you do, comes back to you!" The woman felt irritated. "Not a word of gratitude," she said to herself.

"Everyday this hunchback utters this jingle! What does he mean?" One day, exasperated, she decided to do away with him. "I shall get rid of this hunchback," she said. And what did she do? She added poison to the bread she prepared for him. As she was about to keep it on the windowsill, her hands trembled. "What is this I am doing?" she said. Immediately, she threw the bread into the fire, prepared another one and kept it on the windowsill.

As usual, the hunchback came, picked up the bread and muttered the words: "The evil you do, remains with you. The good you do, comes back to you!" The hunchback proceeded on his way, blissfully unaware of the war raging in the mind of the woman.

One day, as the woman placed the bread on the windowsill, she offered a prayer for her son who had gone to a distance place to seek his fortune. That evening, there was a knock on the door. As she opened it she was surprised to find her son standing in the doorway. He had grown thin and lean. His garments were tattered and torn. He was hungry, starved and weak.

As he saw his mother, he said, "Mom, it's a miracle I'm here. While I was but a mile away, I was so famished that I collapsed. I would have died, but just then an old hunchback passed by. I begged of him for a morsel of food, and he was kind enough to give me a whole bread. As he gave it to me, he said, "This is what I eat everyday. Today, I shall give it to you, for your need is greater than mine." As the mother heard those words, her face turned pale.

She leaned against the door for support. She remembered the poisoned bread that she had prepared in disgust for that hunchback that morning. Had she not burnt it in fire, it would have been eaten by her own son, and he would have lost his life! It was then that she realized the significance of the words: The evil you do remains with you; the good you do, comes back to you!

The Debts of Past

You are alone, you have no companion; you will suffer the consequences of your own deeds.

—Kabir Das

A common leader may not understand the power of nemesis, but leaders with Sufi Sagacity understand the life principles clearly and profoundly. They are guided by the life principles—the law of energy responses. The justice of life is the greatest justice. Leaders must trust them and lead. Life principles are simple—anything which is sordid, filthy, lustful, unethical and immoral is not good for the health of life. We demand many things from life but never bother to find, 'What does Life demand from us?' But, life does not demand in a loud voice. It only whispers mildly. It whispers what it wants from you. Its whispers are so faint that most of us do not hear what it says. Some hear the whispers of their soul but ignore them, as these are not loud enough.

If you can only see what the light reveals to your eyes and hear only what the sound announces to your ears, you are neither seeing nor hearing. The signals of light and sound can be seen and heard even by animals. Man is definitely superior to animals—far superior. Man possesses more sophisticated faculties. Yet most of us do not trust them. We mostly prefer to rely upon the animal faculties—*five sensory perceptions*. If human beings, like animals, rely only on the five sensory perceptions, they lose the benefit of the *divine gift* exclusively given to human beings. Once we start relying upon our animal instincts, we begin to lose our human dignity; there are some who even lose their human identity. Instincts are stronger in animals than human beings. When we make a wrong choice, we live a life poorer than an animal's.

We demand many things from life. We believe that life is meant only for giving and we do not owe anything to it in return. What a selfish approach! Life gives us some things expecting certain returns. It does not demand; it mildly suggests. It states or refers to something as a possible choice or course of action. It reminds subtly. Since our ears are tuned to hear the loud timepiece-alarms or the noisy buzzing sound of the organisers or cell phone alarms, we do not pay any heed to those silent reminders. Yet life never makes a noise. Making noise is not in its nature. But it gives us the rewards and punishments based on the choices that we make while leading the life.

If life were only the *giver* and not the *taker*, there would not have been any obligations upon human beings. Then it would hardly matter whether you love people or hate and kill them. If you hate and kill, others would hate and kill you. No shame or guilt on either side. We, however, sensitise guilt each time we do something which life forbids us from doing. *Guilt* is a precious divine gift to mankind. It is guilt that creates the feeling of penitence upon sins and misdeeds. There are many sinful deeds that are not punishable as per the law of many lands. Yet people feel the guilt. They feel penitent. Why? It is because we know we have violated and deviated from the path that life wanted us to follow. Even those who do not believe in the Creator or the human soul suffer from such guilt. It is they who mostly commit suicide. Those who believe and realise their obligations towards life sincerely repent and seek apologies from the Life Giver. They correct their course of action and try to follow their life obligations—the prescriptions and proscriptions.

Leaders who understand and trust the universal law of energy response move from head to heart and transcending to higher level of consciousness.

Life in this world is a *mountain echo*—what you shout, you hear. What you sow, so you reap. So, do good things and don't ever stop doing *good turns*, even if the beneficiaries do not appreciate it. Don't hope for returns. Returns are bound to come back, if not in this world but surely in the Hereafter you are going to get compensation for your actions. The evil you do remains with you; the good you do, comes back to you. These laws are perfect and eternal.

Leaders who possess Sufi Sagacity understand the life truth—*consequences of our actions*! You hear what you shout. You get what you give. You reap what you sow. Your thoughts and actions are the seeds that you sow! Many leaders

Trust Life Principles...

How can I lose faith in the justice of life, when the dreams of those who sleep upon feathers are not more beautiful than the dreams of those who sleep upon the earth?

—Kahlil Gibran, *The Greatest Works of Kahlil Gibran*

have suffered, many are suffering and many shall suffer—the cosmic principles are eternal. Learn to have faith in the justice of life.

God has given the man *Free Will*. We make the choices and face the consequences. 'In each act is your choice,' says Osho, 'and on each step you can change the very direction of your life.' Osho strongly believes in Nemeses—as you sow, so shall you reap, if not in this world, in the next world. 'For a wicked the next world is the siege of fire; for the pious, the siege of roses.' The life we live is a rehearsal of the life that we would liver eternally.

> ## This Life Is a 'Rehearsal'
>
> Even in death, a man who understands finds tremendous thankfulness towards existence, because for him death is a rest—for him death is not the end of life but the beginning of a far greater life than this one. This was just a rehearsal of the real life—it was not real
>
> —Osho, *The Inner Journey*

Understanding of this truth will make us humble before life and people whom we lead.

If the leader acquires ill-gotten wealth, he suffers—the scams will never allow him to live in peace. If the leader is an honest person yet suffers, let him have patience; the Universal Law of Energy Response shall work and provide protection and reward in the long run. 'Don't grieve,' consoles Rumi, a great Sufi, 'Anything you lose comes round in another form'.[1] When God shuts one door, He opens many doors for you but unfortunately we go on knocking the one that is closed for your goodness.

We choose our joys and sorrows long before we experience them. Nemeses do work in corporate life as they work in our life. As mentioned earlier, the *corporate world* is not an alien staying somewhere out of this world. It is a part of the same world we live in. So, no different cosmic principles bind our corporate life.

The laws of consequences are so perfect that we can see the future by understanding the past. You cannot grow apples by sowing

---

[1] Jelaluddin Rumi, *RUMI Daylight—A Daybook of Spiritual Guidance*.

the seeds of jackfruit. You know it because when last time you grew the jackfruit seeds, apples were not grown. Omar Khayyam, whose love for God was mistaken for love for women and wine, was in fact a Sufi with great wisdom and a great mathematician, scientist, astronomer, philosopher and poet, who was born on 15 May 1048 and died on 4 December 1131. He explains the *law of consequences* in simple words: 'When I want to understand what is happening today or try to decide what will happen tomorrow, I look back.' If false has failed in past, sooner or later it will surely fail in future; if truth has succeeded in past, sooner or later it shall succeed in future. What we say *fate* is the consequential results of our actions in the past in this very life. Omer Khayyam explains the law of energy response this way: 'The moving finger writes, and having written moves on. Nor all thy piety nor all thy wit, can cancel half a line of it'.[2]

Picture the following.

> **Accumulated Yields of Deeds**
>
> When you accumulate virtue with continued practices, you do not see the good of it, but in time it will function; if you abandon right and go against truth, you do not see the evil of it, but in time you will perish.
>
> —Zen Saying

It was a momentous day for a big corporate giant. The CEO was signing a multi-million dollar contract for a turnkey project. The project and marketing guys were jubilant. The CEO and others did not realise that this *contract* was fated to be given to this company the day it had handed over a turnkey project successfully to another client company a few years back. Today's event was not the beginning but the end result of their earlier success—*we choose our joy and sorrow long before we experience them.*

'We often borrow from our tomorrows to pay debts to our yesterday,' wrote Kahlil Gibran, more than a century ago.[3] What we

---

[2] Omer Khyyam, *Omer Khyyam's Rubiyat.*

[3] Kahlil Gibran, *The Greatest Works of Kahlil Gibran.*

see happening today, good or bad, is just a response to the stimulus of yesterday. No action is complete unless the *reaction of the action* takes place. If you sow the seeds of values and virtue, you will reap the harvest of profit that will benefit both your life and business; if you choose to earn money by dubious means, you will still make a profit but that profit will not enrich your life and business. Over time, you will reap the results of your deeds.

Likewise, when a company loses a contract, that loss was fated to it on the day it had displeased another company due to its lack of competence or commitment or for employing some dubious means. We reap what we sow—good or bad.

Between *stimulus* (action) and *response* (reaction) there is a space—the space of time. In that space is our power to choose our response. And in our response lies our growth, success or failure. What we get today was decided by the *choice* of our response yesterday. Our choices decide the outcome. God has written our destiny with the ink of choices that we make to respond to a situation. God has given us a *free will* and guided us in clear terms to choose *what is right* and *what is wrong*! Good deeds or bad deeds are like seeds that we sow in the soil of destiny. They grow and give us the fruits—healthy or poisonous!

When we get a lucrative business contract we feel happy and when we lose, we feel bad. However, what we do not understand or realise is that our fate in winning or losing the present business contract was decided and frozen long back when we had handled or mishandled a project, supplied a good or bad product, or provided a service satisfying or discomforting to a customer.

Our success lies in making the right choices while facing a situation; each choice has its predetermined consequence(s). The Law of Energy Response does work in our personal life. It also works in business as well as in leadership! Understanding of this reality would make the leaders virtuous and the led, sober.

It pays to plan ahead. It wasn't raining when Noah built the ark.

—*Unknown*

13

BUILD THE ARK FIRST

Start a huge, foolish project, like Noah...it makes absolutely no difference
what people think of you.
— JELALUDDIN RUMI, *RUMI DAYLIGHT*
—*A DAYBOOK OF SPIRITUAL GUIDANCE*

Relations are delicate. They need to be handled with utmost care. When it comes to handling Industrial Relations (IR), we must know that they are very fragile. It takes time to build harmonious industrial relations but a single mishandling of an IR situation can spark fire. B.L. Verma, my boss in CCI, taught me many IR mantras. Once he said, 'Siddiqui, today I am giving you the Gayatri Mantra for Managing Industrial Relations: *Hope for the best; prepare for the worst.*' I have etched this in stone. I used this mantra not only for managing industrial relations but also all sorts of relations, including human relations. Relationships are delicate. One must handle them with utmost care.

The other guru mantra that I learnt from P.C. Neogy, CMD of HMT, is equally precious. He used to guide me: 'Work hard at your *Private Stage* to get best results at your *Public Stage*.' These two mantras formed my work habit. I never leave things on chance. I always do well my homework.

Don't Spoon-feed

All life demands struggle. Those who have everything given to them become lazy, selfish, and insensitive to the real values of life.

—Pope Paul VI

Both preparedness to face any unexpected situation and hard work at private stage are important. Leaders must render guidance to their people but should never give solutions on platter. If you addict your people by serving solutions on the platter, then don't blame them for lack of initiative and proactive approach. Leaders must know that God asked Noah to build the Ark first then only He saved him and his people from Deluge—the great flood.

There are two ways to look at God's help: (a) *Life gives the best to those who leave the choice to God*; and (b) *God helps those who help themselves*. These two statements seem to be dissimilar but in fact are complementary. They are not paradoxical; rather, they are the two faces of the same coin.

The dreams that you see in your waking hours are the vision shown by God to help you. But dreams without your actions make no sense. Once you put your best foot forward, God's blessings start showering on you. If you do not succeed, He provides another opportunity to you. If *yesterday* did not end up the way you had planned, God has created *today* for you to fulfil your dreams. One must see a dream. One must muster courage to dream high. The dream must be seen in wakefulness. Not sound sleep but sleeplessness fulfils the dreams of daydreamers.

Dream *Realities*

A dream doesn't become reality through magic; it takes sweat, determination and hard work.

—Collin Powell

An ancient parable stands true even today; it is bottomless deep in meaning. It appears a man dreamed a dream, and when he awoke, he went to his soothsayer and desired that his dream be made plain unto him. And the soothsayer said to the man, 'Come to me with dreams that you behold in your wakefulness and I will tell you their meaning. But the dreams of your sleep belong neither to my wisdom nor to your imagination.' The daydreams seen in our wakefulness are better than the dreams that we see in deep slumber.

A dream without action is the dream that you see in slumber. The dream supported by action makes the things happen. A dream of a visionary leader creates prosperity for the entire nation. 'The angels know that too many practical men eat their bread with sweat of the dreamer's brow,' says Kahlil Gibran.[1] A visionary leader dreams and supports it with planned actions. A vision without action remains a dream, which is of no worth.

A Sufi's story provides great wisdom to those who understand the softer aspects of life:

In a small town on the bank of a river, there lived a pious Sufi. Once during a storm, the river was in spate and the town was flooded. People ran around in panic trying to reach some ground at a height to protect themselves. The water rose quickly in all the streets, and began to flow into houses. When the Sufi saw what was happening, he said to himself, "I have served God faithfully all my life, and surely he will save me from drowning. I shall not flee along with others but stay right here and wait for Him to rescue me." So the Sufi climbed to the roof of the house and prayed, "Oh God, I have trust in you. Save me," and waited for Him to do something.

Soon afterwards, a man came by in a boat and offered to take him to safety. But the Sufi shook his head and said, "No, no… don't worry, God will save me."

Steadily the water rose higher. Then, a motor-boat loaded with people came by and a man urged him to join them. "No, no… don't worry, God will save me," he said, again.

Soon the water was up to his shoulders and still rising. This time, the people passing by in a raft came to his help. But he waved them away and said, "God will save me. He will never let me down."

[1] Kahlil Gibran, *The Greatest Works of Kahlil Gibran.*

The house was soon submerged in water and the Sufi drowned. When he went to Heaven, he looked at God and asked, "How could you have done this to me when I trusted you with all my heart and served you faithfully? Why didn't you do anything to save me?"

"Umm!" said God "Who do you think sent those three boats?"

God helps those who help themselves.

A few tribal people came to Prophet Mohammad on camels to seek his audience. The holy prophet asked them *what they had done to their camels*. They replied, 'Oh Holy Prophet, we left our camels untied, trusting that God will protect them.' The Prophet asked them to go back and tie the camels and said, 'First *you* perform your duty, then leave things to God.'

God had asked Noah to build the Ark before He saved him and his people from the great Deluge.

Leaders of expanded consciousness not only foresee the future but also stay in preparedness. Nothing can surprise them. Only those who build their Arks can survive in the great deluges.

One cannot learn from someone whom one distrusts.

—Idries Shah

14

LEADER AND THE LED

Let there be spaces in your togetherness; and let the winds of the heavens dance between you.
—KAHLIL GIBRAN, *THE GREATEST WORKS OF KAHLIL GIBRAN*

I have served many bosses; some of them were very effective leaders. One such leader was H.R. Alva, my Director Personnel, who was quite humble. He was very friendly but highly demanding. He used to speak in low tone but we always took his words as commands. We were very friendly to him, but in intimacy he used to maintain a distance. No one could ever take chance with him. He was reserved but very open and receptive. Later, when I read *The Greatest Works of Kahlil Gibran* I realised that Alva's relationship with his juniors was akin to what Kahlil Gibran, the Sufi of Lebanon, had envisaged.

The leader and the led should be close to each other but uniquely distancing themselves. It is delicate but not impossible. One can learn from the mother-cat's catch. She holds her baby firmly without piercing her teeth into baby's skin. Likewise the leader and his people should be together but there should be a space in the togetherness. Kahlil Gibran explains this delicate relationship between the leader and the led ones with his poetic fervour:

> *Give your hearts, but not into each other's keeping,*
> *For only the hand of Life can contain your hearts.*
> *And stand together yet not too near together;*
> *For the pillars of the temple stand apart,*
> *And the oak tree and the cypress grow not in each other's shadow.*[1]

So, create a space in between yet remain in togetherness.

Create Intimate Distance...

Love one another, but make not a bond of love;

Let it rather be a moving sea between the shores of the souls;

Fill each other's cup but drink not from one cup.

Give one another of your bread but eat not from the same loaf.

Sing and dance together and be joyous, but let each one you be alone,

Even as the strings of lute are alone though they quiver with the same music.

—Kahlil Gibran, *The Greatest Works of Khalil Gibran*

Someone once asked Sheikh Saadi, a Sufi from Sheraz to explain relationship between the leader and the led. 'Is it like between two brothers or between two friends?' he asked. Sheik told that the relationship between the leader and the led is like two friends. Upon this the man asked, 'What is the difference between a *brother* and a *friend*?' Sheikh replied, 'Brother is like gold and friend is like diamond.' The person wondered and asked again how Sheikh preferred a friend over brother, comparing him with diamond which is far precious than gold. Sheik explained: 'If there appeared any crack in the gold then it could be melted and reshaped as per its original

---

[1] Kahlil Gibran, *The Greatest Works of Kahlil Gibran*.

shape, whereas if there appears a crack in the diamond, it could never be reshaped to its original shape.' What Sufi meant was simple. In blood, relationship one can patch up easily. But where there is no blood relation, it is difficult to *forgive and forget*. The crack remains forever. Likewise, once there is mistrust between the leader and the led, it lasts forever.

Another Saint, Swami Rama, compares the leader (guru) and the led with the boat and the travellers, when the journey is over the boat is no more needed.

Leader (Guru) is not the goal or destination. Anyone who establishes himself as the guru to be worshipped is not a guru. Leader (guru) is like a boat for crossing the river. It is important to have a good boat and it is very dangerous to have a boat that is leaking. The boat brings you across the river. When the river is crossed the boat is no longer necessary. You don't hang onto the boat after completing the journey, and you certainly don't worship the boat.

Alas! Many do not understand this distinction and worship the boat.

If one takes the kernel from the Sufi thought, he will gain wisdom that the role of a leader to get the task accomplished. Once it is over, the leader's purpose is fulfilled and let the led be happy and gain the benefit. This Sufi wisdom reflects from the famous Buddhist belief: 'When you see Buddha on the road, kill him.' It means follow the teachings and guidance of Buddha but don't get attached to the person (Buddha). Teachings are important. One should follow those teaching and should not start worshipping the teacher.

What Swami Rama mentioned recently about leader (guru), the same thought you will find with Lao Tzu, the Old Master of 500 BC era, who said, 'When his (leader's) task is accomplished, without unnecessary speech, his work is done. People say, "We did it!"'.[2]

In India, Mahatma Gandhi comes true to the profile of the leader described by Lao Tzu. He guided the masses and led the

[2] Lao Tzu, *Tao Te Ching.*

country and didn't give up until we the Indians won freedom by breaking the shackles of slavery. Once the task was accomplished, he withdrew from the active politics and allowed others to collect and distribute the fruits of freedom. He happily rested in his ashram with his Charka. I do not find an analogous example for corporate leadership. Contrarily, many famous CEOs attain popularity by appointing PR agencies.

Maintaining relationship with the juniors is an art. If you keep distance, you lose intimacy. If you become too intimate, the required space cannot be maintained. So, maintain an *intimate distance* with your followers. Guide them but don't hog their credit. Walk your talk.

The followers see not what did the leader preach but what he practice. Not *bhashan* and speeches but your actions should render guidance. A leader who cannot walk his talk cannot inspire his followers. Be very intimate with your people, yet maintain some distance! How? Learn from a 'Mother Cat'!

Within tears, find hidden laughter;
Seek treasures amid ruins.

—Rumi

15

BE A MELODY MAKER

*When you reach the heart of life you will find yourself not higher than
the felon and not lower than the prophet.*
—KAHLIL GIBRAN, *THE GREATEST WORKS OF KAHLIL GIBRAN*

On one of the festive occasions I had an opportunity to meet an old timer, one of the former directors of HMT. I couldn't resist asking a question that was creating a noise in my mind for many years.

'*Sir, in your days there were no management institutes in India. None of you possessed any professional qualifications, yet HMT was managed so well that you people gave one new factory every year to nation. HMT was on its zenith. Today we have countless MBAs at various levels including top team, yet we are sweating and the company is profusely bleeding?*' I asked. He patiently listened and gave a brief reply.

'*Yes, we didn't know how to manage? But we knew how to create melody in the hearts of our people. We didn't manage; we simply created symphony.*'

Amazing! Those were the days when the melody was queen.

For a loving heart life is a love song; for the heart filled with hatred, life is nothing but cacophony.

When you reach the heart, you listen an unsung melody. Life is music. Life is a melody. A leader must know how to create melody that comforts the heart and soothes the soul. Music that strums *eternal* notes comes when the musical strings of the heart are neither too tight nor too loose. There is a state when the strings are neither tight nor loose—the midpoint. Music arises there. Buddha, therefore, always pleaded for the middle-path; so too advised Prophet Mohammad and Jesus Christ. Hinduism also stands for moderation and wholesomeness.

Extremism is not akin to life's melody. Extremism is required only for a revolutionary change. Moderation in life yields better results. Revolutionary change is not needed at every cockcrow. Such need is felt once or twice in a lifetime.

Extremism is good to revolutionise the society, not otherwise. Water transforms into vapour at the extreme high (boiling) temperature; water transforms into ice at the extreme low (freezing) temperature. Remember, only if there is an extreme development can there be a transformation. All transformations take place at extreme points. No transformation takes place below that. If water is heated, it does not evaporate when it is lukewarm. Lukewarm water remains water. It turns into vapour only when it is heated to an extreme point. But do we need such extreme points every day?

Coming to transformation in human life we must first understand that such *extreme points* are not external, they are internal. *Awareness* is the seed of transformation in human life. It is awareness that creates the awakening. This way, transformation in life takes place in your heart—what is commonly called a *Change of Heart*. Such a change of heart should come through extreme love and not through extreme hatred. Violence and terrorism can never create the desired change of heart. Such a change comes only through love and passion.

'How stupid is he who would patch the hatred in his eyes with the smile of his lips!' Kahlil Gibran who was born with a Sufi heart is very correct—you cannot create harmony through a 'toothpaste ad'; smile while your heart is filled with hatred. 'If your heart is a volcano how shall you expect flowers to bloom in your hand?' he asks.

Your attitudes play a vital role in creating music in your life. You cannot be optimistic about life through pessimistic eyes. Likewise, you cannot hear the melody of life through pessimistic ears. Life is a mountain's echo—what you shout you hear. Likewise, when you love your followers, they love you in return. When you trust them, they would trust you. When you create melody in their life, they sing a chorus lifting your status higher than you could have ever imagined. Lean towards them but don't bend; be very close to them, maintaining an invisible distance. Be together, but not too near in togetherness. Maintain a good balance—the melody is created with the combination of high and low musical notes.

> **Genuine Smile**
>
> I love smiles. That is a fact. How to develop smiles? There are a variety of smiles. Some smiles are sarcastic. Some smiles are artificial—diplomatic smiles. These smile do not produce satisfaction, but rather fear or suspicion. But a genuine smile gives us hope, freshness. If we want a genuine smile, then first we must produce the basis for a smile to come.
>
> —Dalai Lama, *The Path to Tranquility*

Living life successfully involves maintaining a life-balance all through. It is a difficult task. Maintaining balance between two extremes is difficult but there rests the success. A thin line separates a genius from the insane: both are unreasonable and they challenge the man made laws. Both try to create melody, but the only problem with the insane is that his musical instrument is slightly out of tune.

Unfortunately the world as well as the corporate world has no interest in your love energy. Its whole interest is in your head—in your logical capacity—because that can be used as a commodity in the market.

Soul is known through the heart; the truth is known through the heart. Only a loving heart can touch the heart of life. Love is nothing but the humming of the heart. The heart is the centre from where both the emotional and spiritual energies flow. Only through the human heart can one reach the heart of life. In the heart where love lives, hatred cannot dwell. In a heart that has pure love, hatred becomes impossible.

As mentioned earlier, the heart filled with pure love carries no space for fear and hatred. It carries only *passion*. The one who loves with a pure heart does not know how to hate. He knows only *passion*. Love and hate cannot coexist in the same heart.

Pure love is the catchphrase! *Pure love* expressed in action is *passion*. Loving mankind is creating melody. But loving mankind is not enough; one should love all creatures to create great melody. 'When a man has pity on all living creatures then only is he noble,' believes Omar Khayyam.[1] It is possible when your heart knows how to create the melody for your soul.

Therefore, the heart should always be filled with *love* and *passion*. This is extremely necessary; this should be the priority. But if love is not pure, it takes no time to turn into hatred. In an ordinary heart, love and hatred live together. Only when love becomes pure, like Sufi Rabiya's love for God, does hatred disappear. Mostly a bad person is hidden in a good person and a good person is hidden in a bad person. In Indian tradition, the examples of Angulimal and Valmiki are the models before us. They were the bad guys—one was wicked and cruel, and the other, unaware and ignorant. But when wisdom dawned, they changed and outshone the Sufis, saints and godly persons. They killed the *inner* bad person, once and for all.

Melody comes from harmony, what we get from discord is noise. Life loves melody, not discord. Melody makers are true leaders. In fact, they are bellwethers who reach people through the route of their hearts and get their best.

[1] Omar Khayyam, *Omar Khayyam's Rubaiyat*.

The more rules you make, the more thieves are created!

—Lao Tzu

16

THE ART OF 'WU WEI'

A great tailor cuts little.

—LAO TZU, *TAO TE CHING*

I was sponsored to the UK for three months, where, inter alia, I also conducted studies on Performance Appraisal System as an effective tool for creating the culture of excellence. I returned like Moses, holding in my arms the tablets of *Commandments for Excellence*.

My Director asked me to modify the performance appraisal system of HMT, using new inputs. A team was constituted. We worked hard and developed a new system—Performance Improvement & Development System (PIDS). We were very enthused with our new product. But when we made a presentation before the Board, the unexpected resistance came from our own Chairman, M.R. Naidu.

'Why at all should there be rules or systems for developing a culture of excellence?' He raised the fundamental objection.

'Systems help attain the required objectives and they are capable of creating the desired climate,' was my response. Then I once again explained the highlights of the proposed system. He simply smiled. Perhaps I couldn't convince him.

'How's that some of the best companies of world do not have such systems, yet they have rich culture of excellence,' he argued.

'But, sir, can we compare the work culture of HMT with those world class companies?' I asked. He simply smiled.

Water Logic

The highest good is like water. Water gives life to the ten thousand things and does not strive. It flows in place men reject and so is like the way of Tao.

In business, be competent;
In action, watch the timing!
—Lao Tzu, *Tao Te Ching*

I am not contesting or undervaluing the PIDS as a system—I am merely questioning its utility in practice. Rules regulate and constrict the flow. What I want is something synonymous to the flow of water. Water freely and fearlessly goes deep beneath the surface of things—it flows and helps flow. What I am looking for is something that would stimulate flow as smooth as the flow of water.

He shared his mind. After a brief pause he said, 'However, I am not stopping you. You may try this new system as a dry run, but keep my requirements in mind.'

Though I did not fully comprehend the wisdom of his sermon, I was happy over getting the *let go* for implementation of the systems designed by me. Later, when I read Lao Tzu's *Tao Te Ching* I could understand his lofty expectations of my Chairman—creating a culture of excellence without obstacles or hindrances from rules and procedures! So long we maintain fluidity in our thoughts and approach, creativity goes on designing and forming various patterns as a natural force. Fragility, flexibility, agility and softness maintain the flow, whereas rules and regulations provide rigidity, inflexibility and hardness, which hamper and hinder the natural flow. I understood what Lao Tzu calls 'Wu Wei'. 'Wu Wei' is an ancient Taoist art of living, practised by most of the Chinese monks in good old days. It is also known as 'Wei Wu Wei' (Action Without Action).

Lao Tzu's work mostly reflects Wu Wei—the law of manifestation without or rather beyond human intervention. The art of Wu Wei is based on the universal law of energy response—let cosmic forces play their role. Let happenings dance on the cosmic rhythm. Let things happen without human intervention. Let life unfold and unfurl. Let…

> **Yin Is Powerful**
>
> Yield to over come;
> Bend and be straight.
> Empty and be full;
> Wear out and be new.
> Have little and gain;
> Have much and be confused!
> —Lao Tzu, *Tao Te Ching*

'Wu Wei' is a unique art of leadership. What little I could understand about Wu Wei at my wrong side of fifties was revealed unto me by a pair of sparrows in my childhood.

During my childhood my sister, two years elder, was my guru. She used to take lead and I used to follow her depositing my sincerity at her disposal. We had lots of fun to do for we had lots of time to kid around. My mother was seriously ill and my father's sole objective was to save her life. She was treated in a city hospital and we were brought up in a small town distancing us from our parents. We grew almost without parenthood, though ours was not a broken house.

Once we found a baby sparrow that had fallen from the nest made in the cavity of ceiling. The parent sparrows were perching on the ground making hue and cry trying to inspire the young one to get up and fly. The poor guy was making attempts but was not able to fly.

We were not the guys who would remain silent observers in our mini universe of childhood! We were active players born to make things happen. We immediately decided to help the baby sparrow. My sister took the lead and I obediently followed her. To comfort and warm the baby-sparrow we first kept it in cotton gauze then started making all sorts of abortive attempts to feed it. She twisted a piece of cotton gauze and made a thread, and then she soaked it in milk. I forced open the beak of the baby-sparrow and she attempted pouring drops. The guy resisted but we went forcing our goodness upon it. The parent sparrows were hovering over our head making protest, but not loud enough to sensitize our innocent ignorance.

Then, after some time the parent sparrows decided to abandon their child. They flew away. As one can guess, the baby-sparrow died leaving us wonder struck!

There are certain things in life we must allow to manifest. What we call 'make happen' may sometimes hamper the process and rupture the product.

The other day I received an email from my friend, Charles. He enclosed an attachment—Butterfly. He mentioned, 'The creator of this marvelous text of wisdom requested the Internet surfers to send the message to the friends and show them how much you care.' I 'pay forward' the good-turn that I received from Charles, my cyber friend.

'One day, a small opening appeared in a cocoon; a little boy sat and watched for butterfly for several hours as it struggled to force its body through that little hole.'

'Then, it seems to stop making progress. It appeared as if it had gotten as far as it could and it would not go any after. So the little boy decided to help the butterfly; he took a pair of scissors and opened the cocoon. The butterfly then emerged easily.'

'But the little boy continued to watch because he expected that, at any moment, the wings would open, enlarge and expand, to be able to support the butterfly's body, and became firm. Neither happened! In fact, the butterfly spent rest of its life with withered body and shriveled wings. It never was able to fly.'

'What the little boy, in his kindness and his goodwill did not understand was that the struggle required for that butterfly to get through the tiny opening, with God's way of forcing, fluid from the body of the butterfly into its wings, so that it would be ready for flight once it achieved its freedom from cocoon.'

Allow manifestation! Allow things to happen sometimes. You cannot always make things happen. Both, *action* and *non-action* are important for making progress. But knowing when to act and not to makes all the difference. A true leader knows when to act and when not to act. In life, there's a time to be aggressive and a time to be passive, a time to work and a time to rest, a time to hurry and a time to wait and watch.

> ### Low Is the Foundation of High
>
> Too much success is not an advantage.
> Do not tinkle like jade,
> Or clatter like stone chimes.
> Returning is motion of the Tao.
> Yielding is the way of Tao.
> The ten thousand things are born of being.
> Being is born of 'non-being'.
> —Lao Tzu, *Tao Te Ching*

The art of Wu Wei is *wisdom in practice* that gets you the required patience to wait, watch and allow thing to happen keeping a sharp focus on your objectives. This art enables you to chip in effortlessly without exerting. It lets you make your place and contribution in the *occurring* event naturally.

In simple words, the art of Wu Wei is a Taoist practice of not working *against the grain of things*, of waiting for the right moment without forcing anything unduly. All that you have to do is to remain alert and focused on your purpose, and sooner or later the right opportunity would knock the door, things would start falling in place making way for you to proceed.

> ### Paradoxical Truth
>
> The softest things in the universe
> Overcomes the hardest things in the universe.
> That without substance can enter where there is no room.
> Hence I know the value of 'Non-action'.
> Teaching without words and work without doing
> Are understood by very few.
> —Lao Tzu, *Tao Te Ching*

Both, in life and business, sometimes one must follow the art of Wu Wei, waiting for the right moment and getting into the process effortlessly. It is not *inaction*; it is seeing *action* in *inaction*. It warrants a deeper sense of understanding to fathom this age-old Chinese vista.

Sought for the right moment without forcing anything unduly. Otherwise, you will either be killing a baby sparrow or making the butterfly a withered creature.

The Old Master, Lao Tzu says, 'Managing a country is like cooking small fish. The more you stir them the less their shape can be maintained.' It takes time to understand Lao Tzu's profound philosophy of leadership. But once you understand you are tempted to read his book *Tao Te Ching* again and again. 'The perfect square has no corners; Great talents ripen late; The highest notes are hard to hear; The greatest form has no shape.'

Do little. Manage less to manage better.
'If heaven and earth cannot make things eternal, how is it possible for man?'

—Lao Tzu

I have always found that Mercy bears richer fruits
than strict Justice.

—*Abraham Lincoln*

17

'MAIN HOON NA...' IS EMPOWERMENT

'The group will not prosper if the leader grabs the lion's share of the credit for the good work that has been done.'
—LAO TZU, *TAO TE CHING*

Many corporate leaders talk about *empowerment* without understanding its meaning. Empowerment is leading *Dil Se*. I recall, when I was picked up from one of the factories to corporate office during my assignment in HMT, my new HR boss, M.K. Jaura, gave his first sermon to me in these words:

Moid, this place is new and you will encounter big bosses. Listen. When

Getting Best from Your People

I will tell you what makes a great manager. A great manager has a knack for making ballplayers think they are better than they think they are. He forces you to have a good opinion of your self. He lets you know he believes in you. He makes you get more out of yourself. And once you learn

how good you really are, you never settle for playing anything less than your very best.
—Reggie Jackson

something goes fine, say, 'I have done it' and if it misfires, say 'my boss had asked me to do so'. Take the credit when things go fine; shift the blame to me when things go wrong.

I was looking at him wondering how to respond? Finally, I did not say anything. Let me confess, many a time he took discredit boldly with a large heart when things misfired due to my mishandling of situations. Credit came to me even for the work that was done by my boss. It needs a large heart to give such support to juniors to get best from them. He would assign most challenging jobs to me and when found me shaky, he would simply say, 'Don't bother, Main Hoon Na...' (I am there to support you).

I learnt from my boss a new credo of leadership:

- If something goes wrong, it is my fault.
- If something turns out alright, we did it.
- If something turns out great, you did it.

I had another 'Main Hoon Na' boss, N. Ramanuja, Chairman and Managing Director of HMT. He had taken best from me by giving me some of the toughest assignments, including *closure* of one of the sick factories. While assigning such responsibilities, he would give his full authority and stand like a rock giving his support. He never let me fall.

I call Peter Block as *Mr Empowerment*. It is he who brought the philosophy of empowerment through his book *The Empowered Manager*. In one of the international seminars, I had an opportunity to listen to Peter Block on the philosophy of empowerment. Inspired and convinced by his heart-touching philosophy, I decided to take *Empowerment* as my HR Mission. So I started preaching *Empowerment*. Empowerment got momentum in HMT. My chairman Mr P.C. Neogy asked me to speak to the senior management group. I agreed and did good homework at my *private stage*. After building rapport when I reached to a higher plane, the Director (Finance) pulled me down. He interrupted me and asked a question challenging the very basics. 'You HR guys always try to excite people with new buzzwords. Tell me, how does "empowerment" differ from the age-old business practice of "delegation of power"?' He laughed, and then everyone laughed, following the unwritten rule of management—*when senior laughs, juniors must also laugh*! This way *empowerment* was laughed out.

I felt hurt. I was pulled down from heights and dropped nose down. In utter shock I could not say anything for a minute. The Director (Finance) was still smiling looking at me, waiting for my response to his *brilliant* question. I mustered courage and said, 'Sir, when I am trying to relate *empowerment* and *delegation of power* even remotely, I am not able to find any relationship between the two!' My words were a bit caustic; I broke the hostile silence. The smiles disappeared.

'Sir, the bureaucratic tools cannot be accepted as management philosophy,' after a pause I continued. '*Delegation of Power* is a bureaucratic tool that stands to remind you of your limits, and not powers. You cannot go beyond the defined limitations! If you override them, you violate the rule of the game—the *Laxman Rekha*.'

To my great surprise he became sober and started listening to my sermon with fullest attention, what is called *responsive listening*. 'Empowerment is trust,' I continued. 'A trust that the seniors repose in the juniors to inspire them without any written assurance. It is an understanding that you go ahead, I am there on your back to give you full support.' I went on.

Next morning, the Director (Finance) called me and shared his heart that he was very much convinced with the philosophy of

> **Authentic Empowerment**
>
> When we align our thoughts, emotions and actions, we are filled with enthusiasm, purpose, and meaning.
>
> There is no memory of fear. We are joyously and intimately engaged with our world—the real experience of authentic power.
>
> —Gary Zukav, *The Seat of the Soul*

empowerment. He asked me to conduct workshops for finance people to create a very positive culture.

Trust is the foundation of empowerment. Trust yourself. Trust others. When your juniors trust you, they come to you finding solutions to their problems. When you trust your juniors, they try to live up to your expectations and give their best to you and to the organisation.

Most people mistake empowerment as external power—the power that you get from without. But what is really authentic is *internal power*, which comes when you are inspired. The role of a good leader is to inspire you. You must develop confidence within you first. You must develop trust with you that someone is there to give support and come forward with the helping hand when you look at him for support.

Many mistake *Delegation of Power* as *Empowerment*. The former is a bureaucratic tool, the latter is 'Main Hoon Na...'—trust in leadership. Likewise, *Abdication* is not *Empowerment*. Abdication is passing the buck to the junior without any guidance or support. In empowerment first you judge the capabilities of your people—their competence and commitment. You are supposed to empower only when both are positive. If a person is weak in competence, he needs training and coaching. If a person is negative in commitment, he needs counselling to improve his attitude and behaviour. If a person is weak both in competence and commitment, you have no other option than to control. Once you find your guy is fully competent and totally committed, close your eyes and *empower* him.

Neither 'Delegation of Power' nor 'Abdication' is *Empowerment*. In *delegation of power* you assign authority mechanically as per the rulebook. In *abdication* you shift the buck. In *empowerment* you build trust and give confidence with the unspoken words 'Main Hoon Na...'

*All day I think about it, then at night I say it: 'Where did
I come from, and what am I supposed to be doing?'
I have no idea. My soul is from elsewhere, I am sure of that,
and I intend to end up there.*

—*Rumi*

18

LEAD WITH A SUFI HEART: 'DIL SE'

We are not human beings having a spiritual experience; we are spiritual
beings having a human experience.
—KEN BLANCHARD, *THE HEART OF LEADER*

Treating a sick human being is easy than treating a sick company. When human being becomes sick, it does not sicken the mind of a doctor. But when a company becomes sick, it sickens the mind of the leader (CEO). I have seen many a leader who lose faith in vision, mission and values with a single kneejerk.

When I learnt that a public sector company, Singareni Collieries Company Limited (SCCL), has been brought back to tracks not once but twice, I decided to meet the wizard R.H. Khwaja (former) Chairman and Managing Director—an IAS (intrapreneur) bureaucrat. When human beings become sick they are sent to a hospital and if unfortunately anyone dies he or she is sent to cremation or burial ground. When a public sector company becomes sick, it is referred to Board for Industrial and Financial Reconstruction (BIFR) and mostly this reference is considered as the eventual end of the sick company. Here was the company that was referred to BIFR twice in the year 1992 and 1996, yet it survived. Not only survived but thrived.

'What is the secret of this miracle,' I asked Mr R.H. Khwaja.

'Simple!' was his cool reply. 'I lead Dil Se…' Then he narrated the story of turnaround. 'I am in romance with Singareni and Singarenians,' he concluded. I requested him to write the story of the turnaround, which he did, and I got the honour to be his co-author for the book *The Acrobatics of Change*, published by SAGE (Response Books). Whereas I called my part 'Genetics of Change', he gave name to his part of book 'The Singareni Love Story'. I dedicate the concluding chapter of this book—Lead with a Sufi Heart, *Dil Se*—to Janab R.H. Khwaja, who used this catchphrase during my first meeting with him. (Currently Mr R.H. Khwaja is Secretary, Ministry of Mines, GOI.)

> **Not Words but Actions Pay**
>
> Motivational theories often flounder when impacted by harsh ground realities. I have always believed in the directness of approach complemented by 'practicing' not 'preaching'.
>
> —R.H. Khwaja, *The Acrobatics of Change*

Mr Khwaja's 'Singareni Love Story' reflects the power of heart, yet in today's materialistic world and corporate world leaders allow the mind to dominate and push the heart to the backseat. Leading *Dil Se* has not found its deserved place neither in political nor in corporate leadership. Leaders trust their minds not hearts. Strange!

I believe in *intangibles*—the intangibles get you the tangible results. During my active corporate life I always managed *Dil Se*. Now as a consultant I conduct workshops on management themes with the flavour of spirituality. As an author I write *Dil Se* and find difficult to sell my products to my publishers. Writing about mind-power get you easy sailing; writing about heart is like swimming against the current. I love to swim against the current. A decade back my writings and workshops were considered a bit skewed. Today when the West started suffering owing to *mind-power*, many are leaning towards the heart. Sufi heart is the purest form of heart. Many could not understand the Sufi thoughts during their lifetimes. 'Your mind and my heart will never agree until your mind ceases to live in numbers and my heart in the mist.' Kahlil Gibran paints the picture vividly clear.[1]

Love and *compassion* reside in the heart and *intellects* in the mind. When you join both, it creates what is called *intuitive spark*. Idries Shah, whose contribution in Sufism is highly respected, explains this spark in his Sufi way: 'The union of the mind and the heart creates intuition [intuitive spark], which brings about illuminating, and the development which the Sufis seek, is based upon love.'

> **Spiritual Liberation**
>
> It is the mind in us that yields to the laws made by us, but never the spirit in us.
> —Kahlil Gibran, *The Greatest Works of Kahlil Gibran*

Like human body has a soul, intangible part of gains in business play an important role. Goodwill is intangible which is more important than profit, the tangible part of business. It is *intangible* that gets you *tangible*. Many do not understand the softer aspects of life as well as business. We recognise our body but not the soul—the eternal part of our existence. Rumi reminds us in these words:

You descended from Adam, by the pure Word of God,
but you turned your sight
to the empty show of this world.
Alas, how can you be satisfied with so little?
So come, return to the root of the root
of your own soul.[2]

Management mavens try to measure everything, understanding not that the softer aspects of life cannot be measured with hard tools. Someone started *IQ* (Intelligence Quotient). Others joined

[1] Kahlil Gibran, *The Greatest Works of Kahlil Gibran.*
[2] Jelaluddin Rumi, *RUMI Daylight—A Daybook of Spiritual Guidance.*

the rat race and coined the word *EQ* (Emotional Quotient)! As if it was not enough, many Western management gurus talk about *SQ* (Spiritual Quotient). Later, they changed the meaning of the acronym *SQ* as *Social Quotient*. What they do not understand is that the softer aspects of life like emotions, sociability or spirituality cannot be fully comprehended through language let alone measuring them in terms of *quotients*. There are certain things in the universe that even the sages and Sufis do not understand. The spirit or soul is one such delicate and finer thing, which cannot be fathomed through five sensory perceptions, then how can one dare measure it with hard tools? I do not subscribe to such meaningless measures with a sheepish approach.

> **Fair Is Foul and Foul Is Fair**
>
> If all they say of good and evil were true, then my life is but one long crime.
> —Kahlil Gibran, *The Greatest Works of Kahlil Gibran*

Today you will find many companies standing on their heads. You look anywhere you will find many big business houses standing upside down. Not only our approach is skewed but also our focus is on wrong spots. Not truth but glamorous events find the spotlight-focus. This reminds me one of the anecdotes of Mulla Nasrudin:

A man noticed Nasrudin intently inspecting the ground outside his door.

"Mulla," he said, "what are you looking for?"

"I'm looking for a ring I dropped," Nasrudin replied.

"Oh," the man replied as he also began searching. "Well where exactly were you standing when you dropped it?"

"In my bedroom," Nasrudin replied, "not more than a foot in front of my bed."

"Your bedroom?!" the man asked. "Then why are you searching for it out here near your doorway.

"Because," Nasrudin explained, "there is much more light out here."

Like Mulla searching his ring outside his door, many of us try to search truth keeping in focus wrong aspects of life. As mentioned earlier, we are running fast without even knowing why we are running? We are running heedlessly. The focus of life has lost the focus.

Today, who find most coverage on TV channels? Not those who create worthy news, but those who create thrill, excitement and even horror, find in focus. Not what is important, but what is sensational finds coverage. The entire focus is on *catching people doing wrong*. The camera eye catches wrong doers and the images are flashed on TV. When we see *wrong doings*, many are internally aroused to do similar evil acts. Can we shift the focus and rather catch people doing right? Can the TV channels throw upon them the spotlight?

Those who learn leading *Dil Se* remain humble and modest. They don't harsh whom them lead. They lead their people with kindness. Harsh words hurt. Hurting is hurting whether it is by weapon or by tongue. The bodily wounds heal up soon, but the scar on the heart created by brutal words remains forever. For this reason people say, 'The broken heart can never be rectified.'

Once two men came to a Sufi. One complained against other, accusing him of using foul language for him. The accused admitted his fault and explained that he had already sought apology, but the man was not willing to forgive him. The Sufi after hearing both asked them to come to him the next morning. He asked the accused to bring bagful feathers of the fowl. The next morning when they came, the Sufi took them to a hillock. It was a windy morning. It was difficult for them to stay stable at the top of the hillock. The Sufi asked the accused to open the bag. As soon as the fellow opened the bag, the tiny feathers flew in the air. The Sufi asked the accused to re-gather and put them back into the bag. The person wondered how could that be possible? 'Sir, how can I gather them back? They have already flown away!' replied the accused. The Sufi then said, 'You are right my son. You cannot gather them back.' He paused and said, 'Likewise, the spoken words cannot be swallowed back. Bad words hurt and create a scar on the heart, which cannot be removed, no wonder how many times you say

"Sorry".' Wisdom dawned upon and the accused promised never to hurt people. Then, the Sufi turned to the complainant and asked, 'Do two mistakes make a right action?' He said 'No.' Then, the Sufi told him pointing towards the accused, 'He did a mistake by hurting you by his tongue, and you did another mistake by not forgiving him, knowing well that God loves those who forgive others.' The complainant felt sorry and embraced the accused saying, 'Brother I forgive you and pray Lord to forgive you.'

The spoken words, good and bad, stay frozen in space and time. You are accountable for your words as you are accountable for your actions. Good words create good feelings. Like any energy, *love energy* also needs a medium to transmit. When you say good words and hug someone, two bodies physically meet and create connectivity between two hearts making it possible for love-energy to flow.

Today our corporate world is passing through the Dark Age in real sense. But this darkness is mysterious. 'Darkness within darkness—the gate to all mystery,' believes the Old Master, Lao Tzu. He further says, 'When the country is confused and in darkness, loyal minsters appear'.[3] Like glow worms, many management gurus and leaders appeared to guide us, taking us from darkness to light. Today many leaders believe in 'Managing from the Heart'. Mind may deceive; heart never misleads.

The leaders who lead *Dil Se* are Lao Tzu's *loyal ministers* who appear like glow worms to shed away darkness.

Look Within and Lead

I, you, he, she, we... In the garden of mystic lovers, these are not true distinctions. When all the Temple is prepared within, why nods the drowsy worshipers outside?

—Omar Khayyam, *Omar Khayyam's Rubiyat*

Leadership is not grabbing power; leadership is all about serving people selflessly. Oh power-suckers understand the true meaning of leadership. Don't try to rule over bodies, conquer the hearts of people. Love and help those who look at you—black men and white men, Hindus and Muslims, Christians, Jews and

[3] Lao Tzu, *Tao Te Ching.*

gentiles, and Sikhs and Buddhists, the Dalit and the downtrodden people.

Lead with love, not with hatred. Spread love, not hatred. Help your followers without expecting returns. God has created us all—none else has created us. We belong to the same family of mankind. How can one kill the creature of God, one's own kith and kin? Don't hate one another. Love one another. Human beings are human beings, whether they have black skin or white!

The scriptures say, the Kingdom of God is within man. Killing an innocent man is killing the entire mankind. It is better to live by each other's happiness rather than to live by each other's miseries. In this world there is scope for everyone, rich and poor, and this world can provide a beautiful life for the entire mankind if we learn to live in peace and harmony.

Hypocrisy has become the way of life—we give fake smiles and utter words, which we do not mean. Greed has barricaded the world with hatred. We have developed speed and lost the sense of direction. We are speeding up without any clues. Speed, added with heedlessness, is the sign of

> **Fake Smile Doesn't Heal**
>
> How stupid is he who would patch the hatred in his eyes with the smile of his lips!
> —Kahlil Gibran, *The Greatest Works of Kahlil Gibran*

disaster. Our misguided leadership has already brought the mankind to the tip of cliff—one more wrong step can create disaster to seven billion people.

The greed has poisoned our souls. The soulless technology is not the need of the day. More than technology we need humanity. More than science we need peace. Without peace the quality of life will be violent. The misery upon us is the gift of greed. Shed away greed and hatred, peace and happiness will return. Happiness of people should be the purpose of leadership. Then the world politics will change its pattern. People are not machines. People are not cattle. We all men and women are the children of humanity. We, the silent majority, have the real power. We have power to make this world beautiful. Let us strive to create happiness. Let us create a new world—a decent world.

Hatred and anger cannot bring harmony. Hostile attitudes only serve to heat up the situation. The hostile thoughts of leaders and the led create a hostile collective consciousness, which in turn fill the society with anger and hatred. Everything begins with thoughts. Ill-thoughts lead to sordid actions. Actions are not cruel; cruelty lies in your thoughts. Actions are reflection of your thoughts, except your instincts, which are spontaneous. But instincts mostly belong to animals, not to human beings. Human beings have intuition—so follow your intuitive wisdom. Control your thoughts first. Once thoughts become pure, your actions are bound to be righteous.

The world is beautiful. Don't spoil it. We have lost the way. Greed has overpowered us. We have given this world hatred, bloodshed and miseries. We have made our knowledge cynical. Our thinking has gone skewed. We work like machines and robots. We have no time to think. We have no time to act. We do little for mankind—the genuine beneficiary! Your leadership should aim at *greater happiness for greater number of people*—the mankind.

Today we need harmony more than cleverness. We need kindness and gentleness. We need to shower love and mercy upon people.

Don't rely too much on technology—it is spiritually empty. The wrong usage of technology has brought us closer to death—*just one spark and the world is gone.* It is human mind that has created the technology. Technology has no heart. Technology has no soul. We think through our mind, not through heart. We trust our mind, not our heart. It is time to act through the heart.

Slavery has not vanished from the surface of the earth. It has returned in many forms. *The New World Order* has a plan for massive slavery—a global slavery! We wrongly assume that *imperialism* is dead. It is very much alive. It has simply changed its form. The imperialist forces have become wiser. They have discovered lacuna in their plans. They have understood the fact that it is impossible to rule the masses in foreign countries. But it is possible to rule the masses through their local leadership—their local rulers. This form of imperialism is far more dangerous. Their plans are greedy. They want to rule over the entire world.

Wake up and oppose those forces, not by violence but through solidarity. If mankind unites and creates a collective consciousness against such greed and hatred, both greed and hatred will wipe out from the surface of the earth. If the mankind unites and creates a collective consciousness for peace, peace will return.

Oh mankind! Return to peace. In peace is prosperity. In peace is growth. In peace lies the future of world and mankind. Let us all unite and work for peace. Let us control our minds to control our actions. Let us follow the right means for the right ends. There is no right way to do a wrong thing!

Creating levels of leadership from Level 1 to Level 5 is attaching numbers to leadership, which is a jugglery rather than yardstick. The softer aspects cannot be measured with the hard tools. I said this earlier. Leadership cannot and must not be measured in terms of numbers. It is as nonsensical as measuring *emotional intelligence* through EQ or the spiritual energy with soul quotient (SQ). Hospitality industry has invented a measuring tool *HQ*—Hospitality Quotient! I don't accept them as measuring tools—the softer aspects of life cannot be measured with hard tools. Likewise, *leadership* cannot

Develop Inner Softness...

The shell of the coconut is hard, but the inside is excellent. In accordance with this, remember, that purity inside is what we should aim at.

The jackfruit has a thorny rind, but it is sweet within.

The sugar cane is hard and black outside, but it is well flavoured and sweet within.

Our food owes its flavour to salt.

So the value of a thing depends on its inner qualities; the faults outside should not be a matter to a true seeker?

—Sant Tukaram

be measured in numbers. The quality of leadership depends upon the depth of consciousness. Whether it is expanding or contracting! Leadership can be recognised and appreciated in terms of results, satisfaction and happiness that it creates to those who are led.

Broadly speaking, there are three types of leaders. First category is of those who are in absolute harmony with their inner core—they are very scarce, almost vanished or have become extinct. They are the ones whose thoughts, feelings, sayings and actions are in absolute harmony—what they think, feel, say and act is in congruity. There is no disharmony in their inner and external selves. All prophets, saints and Sufis fall within this category. They are fearless, bold and straight in their actions. There is nothing to fear so they need not pretend or manipulate. They are spiritually inspired—they are led by their souls.

In the remaining two categories are opposite extremes. Some have softer outer core, but from inside they are hard. Their thoughts and actions do not flow from their heart. They grossly misuse their mind—they pretend to be saintly but they are highly deceptive, crooked and wicked. On the other hand, there are some leaders whose exterior is hard but from inside they are soft. They are highly disciplined but their hearts are filled with love and affection for their people. They are highly disciplined and tough yet soft and humble. *Discipline* and *humility* apparently seem to be contradictory characteristics but these are not conflicting attributes. When I say hard outer core, I mean hardness in terms of discipline, law and order, not in terms of brutality or cruelty. The first and last categories of people can lead *Dil Se*, never those who belong to second category, whose outer core is soft but from within they are devilish.

Today the global community is looking for leaders in political arena and corporate sector who can lead with a Sufi heart—*Dil Se*. When such leaders will arise, they will join hands and lead the world towards peace with love. They bring back the global peace.

It is not a dream in divine madness—it is the divine law. The glow worms appear only in thick dark nights.

Could the *nights* be darker than what we have been witnessing today? No, we are passing through the darkest time ever witnessed by mankind. But this darkness is the augury of divine light, which will illuminate the world—*in thick darkness the loyal ministers appear*.

ABOUT THE AUTHOR

Moid Siddiqui is the Managing Director of Intellects Biz, which is highly regarded for its innovative training workshops on management themes. He uniquely blends *business management* with *spirituality*. He is popularly known as *Management Monk*. He is a new age corporate professional with wide-ranging interests in areas such as developing *human potential* to scripting and directing business management films. He is a triple post-graduate in Sociology, Political Science and Social Work & Business Management.

He has served Corporate India in senior- and board-level positions with premier public sector and private sector organisations, which include BHEL, NHPC, CCI, HMT (GM–HR), BEML (Director, HR) and Nagarjuna Group (Executive Vice President). He has also served a Management Institute—Centre for Organization Development (COD)—as Senior Professor. He is the author of fifteen books on management themes, viz., *The Brave New Manager, Management Parables, Intangibles, Honk, Soul Inc., Corporate Soul, The Smart Crow Never Goes Thirsty, The Pygmalion Manager, The Acrobatics of Change, Watch Your Ladder, Who will Bell the Cat?, Enrich Your Personality, In Search of Meaning, 50 Soul Stories* and *Championing the Bosses*.

Mr Siddiqui is one of the rare Indian authors whose spiritual work has found place in the famous 'Chicken Soup' series.

His articles were published in professional journals of high repute, including American Society for Training & Development's journal *Training & Development*. He is the recipient of several awards, including the All India Management Association's Best Management Book Award of 1995–96 for his book *The Brave New Manager*. His other two books *Corporate Soul* (published by SAGE) and *Enrich*

Your Personality were adjudged as the best book (3rd rank) of the year 2005–06 and Commendation Award for the year 2011–12 by Indian Society for Training and Development (ISTD). He has also authored seven books on religion and spirituality.